D1111019

CONTENTS

THE CRUSADERS
WARRIORS OF GOD

Georges Tate

DISCOVERIES
HARRY N. ABRAMS, INC., PUBLISHERS

At the end of the 11th century the Mediterranean region was divided between the Islamic world, Western Christendom, and Eastern Christendom—or the Byzantine Empire. The Islamic and Byzantine East were the seats of flourishing civilizations, while the Christian West languished behind, struggling to emerge from the barbarism into which it had plunged after a series of invasions and economic decline.

CHAPTER I

THE MEDITERRANEAN WORLD ON THE EVE OF THE CRUSADES

The social elite of the Islamic world held cultural gatherings that might feature recitations of poetry in refined settings (opposite), whereas the aristocrats of the West favored more violent activities, such as jousting tournaments (right).

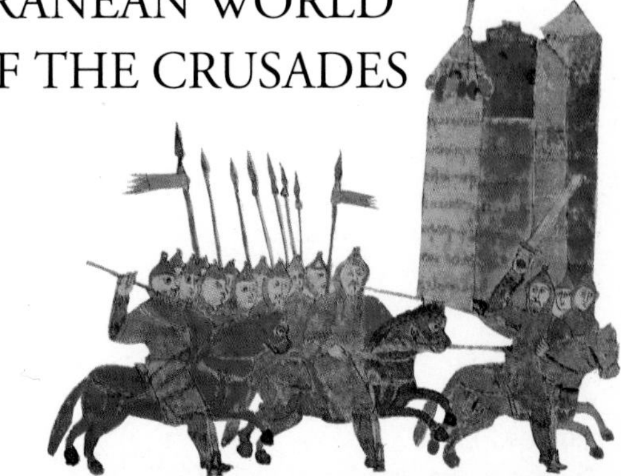

Left: In the cities of the East men gathered at cafés, which served as social centers as well as places to discuss business. Below: Minaret of the mosque of Samarra (in present-day Iraq), a 9th-century Muslim capital city.

The Islamic World Before the Crusaders

Stretching from India to Spain, the Muslim—or Islamic—world drew its unity from the predominance of the Muslim religion and the Arabic language. It boasted splendid cities like Baghdad, Damascus, and Antioch, especially in Syria and Mesopotamia, where the tradition of urban life went back thousands of years. The cities were all laid out along the same design: a mosque and markets in the center of town and, in the principal cities, a ruler's palace; they were surrounded by ramparts and crowned by a citadel. As seats of international or long-distance commerce and centers of regional exchanges, they figured among the largest cities in the world, some with hundreds of thousands of inhabitants. Western cities, by contrast, tended to be administrative and religious settlements, rather than trading centers.

The Caliphate

With the death of the Prophet Muhammad in AD 632, all the

territories bound to Islam were gathered under the authority of a religious and political chief, the caliph. After reaching its zenith under two dynasties, the Abbasids and Fatimids, the caliphate experienced a long political decline. Distant regions seceded to form independent Muslim kingdoms, and Islamic dissidents began to challenge the legitimacy of the caliphs. Of the two main branches of Islam, the Sunni Muslims defended the legitimacy of the Abbasid caliphate, but the Shia Muslims believed that the caliphate should revert to the Imams, descendants of Ali, the Prophet's son-in-law.

In northern Africa the Fatimids, who were Shias, proclaimed themselves caliphs, conquered Egypt, and founded Cairo—which means "victorious" in Arabic—then headed for Baghdad to overthrow the rival Abbasids, who ruled from this city. However, unable to get far enough east, they contented themselves with reaching southern Syria. This was the beginning of a long struggle for control of Syria.

Bold navigators (below), the Muslims extended the range of international commerce and pursued it with an intensity never experienced in antiquity. Discoverers of new lands, they journeyed regularly to India and even to China. Continental trade—over waterways or by caravan—was equally important. The Islamic world, along with Byzantium, constituted an essential trade link between the underdeveloped West and the Far East, between northern Europe and Africa.

The Seljuk Turks

In the mid-11th century a new group of invaders, the Seljuk Turks, swept quickly eastward from Central Asia. Their arrival seemed to promise the restoration of Islamic unity in the Levant, as the eastern shores of the Mediterranean are known. The Turks, who roamed the plains of Central Asia, had converted to Islam in the 10th century. Among them, the Seljuks took on an especially

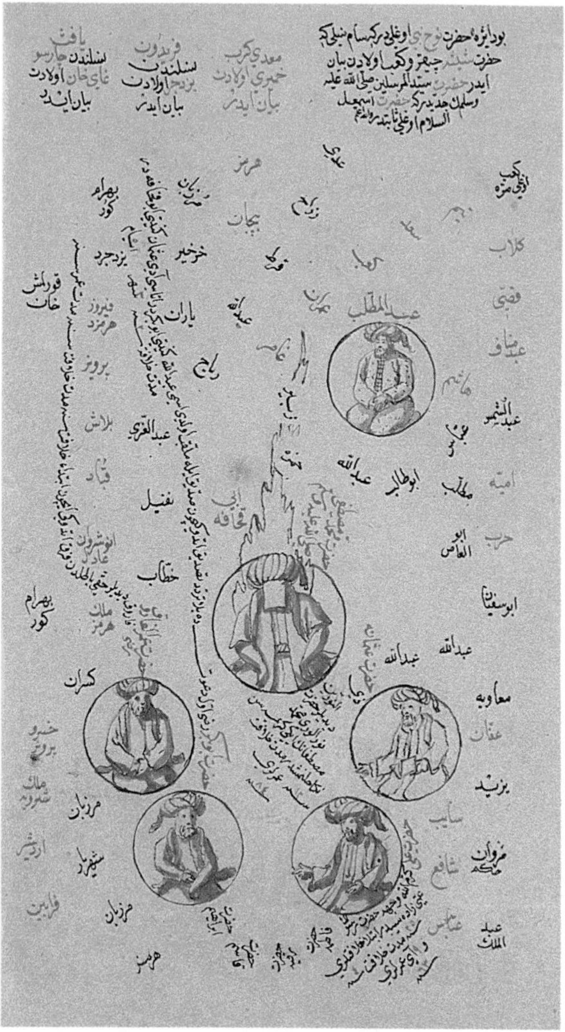

Muhammad's genealogy (left) carries a special importance, for it is the question of his successors and their legitimate claims to power rather than problems of dogma that have set Sunnis, Shias, and Kharijis, and their various branches, against one another. The five principal Islamic duties are the *shahadah*, or "testimony" (the profession of faith stating that Allah is the only god and Muhammad is his prophet), prayer (above), pilgrimage, the fast during the month of Ramadan, and the *zakat* (the generous payment of alms).

important role in the changing political scene of the Levant. In 1055 they seized Baghdad from the Abbasids. Tughril Beg, their leader, imposed his authority on the caliph of Baghdad and awarded himself the title of sultan in order to reestablish the caliphate as a single great

Muslim power. In 1071 they took Jerusalem from the Fatimids.

The Turks Carried Off a Major Victory Over Byzantium at Manzikert in 1071

Later the same year the Seljuks took on the Byzantine Empire at the pivotal battle of Manzikert (present-day Malazgirt, Turkey). Betrayed by some of his own men, Emperor Romanus IV Diogenes was soundly defeated by Sultan Alp Arslan, and the Turks won nearly all the Byzantine provinces of Asia Minor; they stopped just one hundred miles short of Constantinople, the capital of the Byzantine Empire. The loss of Asia Minor was a catastrophe for Byzantium and revealed the powerlessness of the imperial forces in the face of a Turkish menace.

The Seljuks' Attempt to Unify Failed

The Seljuk sultans managed to briefly reunify the Abbasid caliphate under their authority, but they could not subdue the Fatimids. After the death of Malik Shah, who had succeeded his father, Alp Arslan, in 1073, the sultanate fragmented. A bitter battle of succession pitted Malik Shah's brothers against his sons. Baghdad fell to Malik Shah's eldest son, Berkiyaruq. The major cities of the empire were broken up into autonomous emirates governed by *atabegs*, literally "prince-fathers," a Turkish

Far worse than the battle of Manzikert, in which the Turkish Seljuks routed the Byzantine armies, was the subsequent civil war in Byzantium, which brought disaster to the empire. The followers of Romanus IV Diogenes and the army of Asia Minor confronted the forces of the Ducas family and the aristocracy of Constantinople in a fight that benefited only the Turkomans, a fierce band of Turks over whom even the Seljuks had no control. Their tribes plunged deep into Anatolia without encountering resistance (above), eventually resulting in significant changes in the makeup of the population of central Anatolia, with the Turkish element edging out the Greek element, which would have disastrous consequences for Byzantium.

term for the regents of Seljuk princes. Nowhere was this fragmentation worse than in Upper Mesopotamia and Syria, where every town was claimed by a different ruler: Aleppo and Damascus fell to Malik Shah's nephews; Tripoli was ruled by a civilian judge; Shaizar by the Arabic dynasty of the Munqidhites; Mosul by Kerboga; and the region of Diyarbakir by the Ortoqids.

At the end of the 11th century an extreme Shia sect called the Assassins established itself in the Ansariya Mountains in Syria. They were notable not so much for their beliefs as for their deep-seated hostility to Sunnism and their practice of assassination. Their name derived from the Latin word for hashish, the drug used by the Assassins. The "grand master" of the sect exacted absolute obedience from his followers. Sheltered in their "eagles' nests" high up in the mountains, they succeeded in guarding their independence. When it came down to it, the Shias had no intention of helping the Sunnis fight Byzantium or the crusaders—and vice versa.

The citadel of Aleppo (in present-day Syria) is perched on top of a tell —a mound made up of successions of ancient settlements—in the center of the old city (below). In the 12th century the great Muslim leader Nureddin rebuilt the wall and the mosques, built a hippodrome in the center for horse racing, and constructed his "Golden Palace" on the ruins of an old palace.

The Population of Syria

Greater Syria—Syria, Lebanon, and Palestine—comprised a huge array of races and creeds. Many non-Muslims lived in the area, including Jews and Christians. The Jews were scattered throughout the cities of northern Syria and Palestine, although they were particularly numerous in Jerusalem. Among the Christians were Armenians, Greek Orthodox, and Jacobite Syrians, who were the largest group of Christians. The Armenians had been driven out of Armenia by the Greek Church, and the Syrians were considered heretical by both the Greek and the Latin churches. Many Jews and Christians, in fact, felt better off under the Muslims, who largely left them in peace. Such diversity in Syria produced two contradictory effects. On the one hand, it constituted a weakness, since it could cause divisiveness; on the other hand, it fostered tolerance and allowed contacts and associations that were impossible elsewhere at the time.

Aleppo and Damascus were the two largest cities of inland Syria. Since antiquity Aleppo, which fell along the main caravan route across Syria to Damascus, was an important trading center. It briefly flourished as a Byzantine city until the 7th century, when it was taken by Arabs and then Seljuks. The crusaders were determined to take it back, but it held out against repeated attacks.

The Church Divided in Two

By the 4th century AD Rome had fallen and its empire was split into two parts: east and west. The

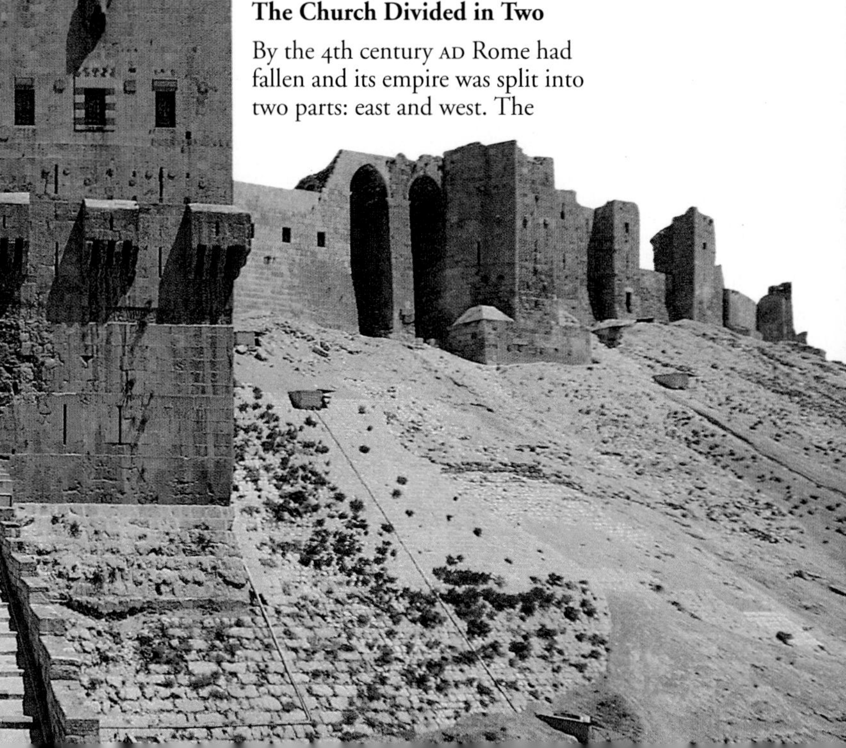

Damascus, capital of the Umayyad dynasty, is believed to be the oldest continuously inhabited city (opposite above).

The European Christians had long been in contact with Muslims in the Islamic country of Spain. They knew that there were still Christians in Spain who had retained their religion and their laws but who spoke Arabic. At the instigation of Pope Gregory VII, who was determined to reform the Church and rid it of "heretical" sects, their liturgy—the Mozarabic rite—was suppressed in 1080 (left, a Mozarabic Bible).

western empire splintered into small states, nominally controlled by the papacy in Rome; while the east, controlled from the city of Constantinople (present-day Istanbul), became known as the Byzantine Empire. Its cultural influences were predominantly Greek (it had once been the site of a Greek colony, Byzantium) and Middle Eastern.

During the early years of the two empires, Rome and

Constantinople competed for religious power. The pope in Rome claimed authority over the entire Christian Church—east and west—while the bishop (patriarch) of Constantinople maintained his dominance over the eastern part of the Church. In 1054, as a result of these power struggles and other theological differences, the Christian Church split into the Roman Catholic—or Latin—Church, headed by the pope in Rome, and the Greek Orthodox Church, led by the patriarch in Constantinople.

The Brilliance of Byzantium's Urban Civilization Masked Its Political Weakness

At the beginning of the 11th century the Byzantine Empire covered all of Asia Minor to Armenia, northern Mesopotamia, and Syria, and included Cyprus, Crete, and the southern Balkans, as well as part of southern Italy. A professional army in the capital of Constantinople, reinforced by divisions of the different

Although the Arabs had captured Jerusalem in 637, they did not prevent Christian pilgrims from visiting the holy sights of the city. They also considered Jerusalem holy since, according to tradition, Muhammad ascended to heaven after praying there at "the Rock." Until 624 the Prophet's followers prayed in the direction of Jerusalem rather than Mecca. Below: Muslim guards at the entrance to the church of the Holy Sepulcher let in Christian pilgrims.

timars, or districts, guaranteed the defense of the empire. Over this immense area reigned the emperor, or *basileus*, direct heir of the Roman emperors. The Byzantine emperor was considered the elected official of God, the supreme agent of justice on earth. In practice, he was as powerful as the conditions of the time allowed. His administration formed a network meant to connect all the elements of society to the empire. In reality it did not work well, as the empire was vast and travel between the different regions was slow.

In the mid-11th century the cities of the empire enjoyed a renaissance, and Constantinople, exceptional in every respect, had close to half a million inhabitants—that is, half the population of Islam's Baghdad. It stood out by virtue of the splendor of its monuments: churches, palaces, sumptuous mansions, and centuries-old ramparts that had turned back tides of invaders. Constantinople was the cultural, economic, and social center of the empire. Its merchants had made it the crossroads of the medieval world, linking it to Islam, the barbarian West, and the plains of Russia.

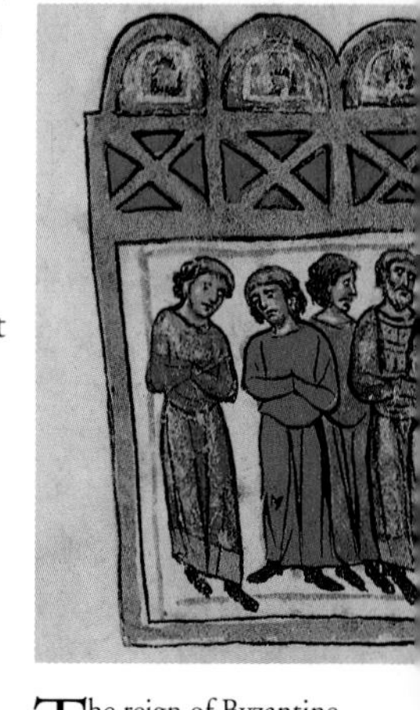

The reign of Byzantine Emperor John II Comnenus (1118–43)—shown with Empress Irene Ducas on the icon below—was marked by great success in foreign affairs. In Asia he conquered Cilicia and Armenia. In Europe he imposed his power on the Petchenegs (nomadic Turks who had threatened Constantinople) and on the Serbs, and he checked the Hungarians.

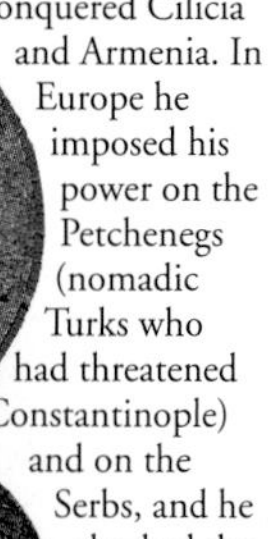

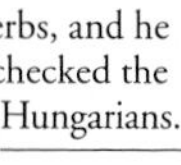

A Short-Lived Peace in Byzantium

For the sake of economic prosperity the Byzantine Empire tried to maintain a state of peace. The emperors stopped their land conquests, dissolved the local armies of the *timars*, and opened imperial positions and honors to the children of the new urban bourgeoisie, who were educated in universities. However, invaders were soon pressing at the frontiers: Normans from southern Italy to the west and Muslims to the east. With relative ease, the Turks overran Asia Minor to the sea of Marmara.

In 1081 Byzantine Emperor Alexius I Comnenus, scion of a great Asian family, took power and countermanded the policies of his predecessors by barring the bourgeoisie from commerce and finance. In order to reconquer the territory lost to the Muslims, he requested soldiers from the pope. He saw no ambiguity or shame in this request to Rome: He was asking for mercenaries, not the intervention of western armies. Only six months later, based in part on the plea from Alexius, Pope Urban made his famous appeal which was to result in the First Crusade.

Constantinople's hippodrome, site of sporting and political events, could hold thirty thousand spectators. The emperor gauged his popularity by the greeting he received from the public, a practice that carried its risks. The people of Constantinople were divided into two factions: the Greens and the Blues—"sporting clubs" that had taken on political ramifications; their coalition in 532 almost cost Justinian his throne. Since then the emperors took care to control the "circus factions." Above: An Arab horseman demonstrates his riding skills. The scene took place in the 8th century, while Constantinople was fighting the Arabs; even war did not prevent such entertainments from continuing.

The Byzantines and Muslims

At the beginning of the 10th century Patriarch Nicholas the Mystic wrote to a Muslim emir that two sovereignties existed: "that of the Saracens [Muslims] and that of the Romans, who flood the whole of the Earth with their light. Thus, it is necessary to live together in brotherhood; having different ways of life, rules of behavior, and religions does not mean they must be inimical toward one another." Through ties of commerce in peacetime, a kind of bond existed between Byzantines and Muslims. When it came to westerners, however, the Byzantines felt they were treated with condescension and mistrust. Indeed, the Latin Church continued to believe that Eastern and Western churches would once again be united under the papacy. In 1055 the papal legates in Constantinople excommunicated Patriarch Michael Cerularius. This action was aimed solely at the person of the patriarch, not at the Greek Orthodox Church. However, in order to justify the seizure of Constantinople by the crusaders in 1204, nearly two centuries later, the papacy retroactively transformed this incident into a schism. Even more serious than that symbolic event were the constant misunderstandings that set Byzantines against westerners.

The Barbarian West

Compared with the East, the West seemed like a barbarous world; however, great changes were in the air. At the end of the 10th century the West was sparsely populated; its peasants were backward and oppressed. The best architecture it had to offer was castles made of wood; it had no money in circulation; waves of invaders had devastated the land; and its cultural life was restricted to the courts of princes and monasteries. The powers of authority were crumbling, and brutality held sway in social relations.

By 1050 the Byzantine Empire stretched from Italy to eastern Anatolia, and from the Black Sea to Lebanon (map, opposite above). It maintained cordial relations with the Fatimid caliphate, while the Abbasid caliphate was paralyzed by its own dissensions. The empire established peace and encouraged the economy. But starting in 1071 the Near East underwent a rapid transformation. Attacked by the Turks and greatly weakened, Byzantium lost most of its Asian territory, while the Turks, under Malik Shah, reunited an immense empire comprising Iran, Anatolia, and the entire Near East except for Egypt, which remained in the hands of the Fatimids. After Malik Shah died in 1092, his son divided the empire once more, creating five large territories. His government was based in Persia, its capital in Baghdad; his brother ruled eastern Persia; his nephews were named princes of Aleppo and Damascus in Syria; and the western portion of Anatolia was entrusted to Kilij Arslan, the eastern half to the Danishmends, a Turkish dynasty. On the eve of the crusades, the Byzantine Empire had greatly contracted, while the Islamic Empire had greatly expanded (map, opposite below).

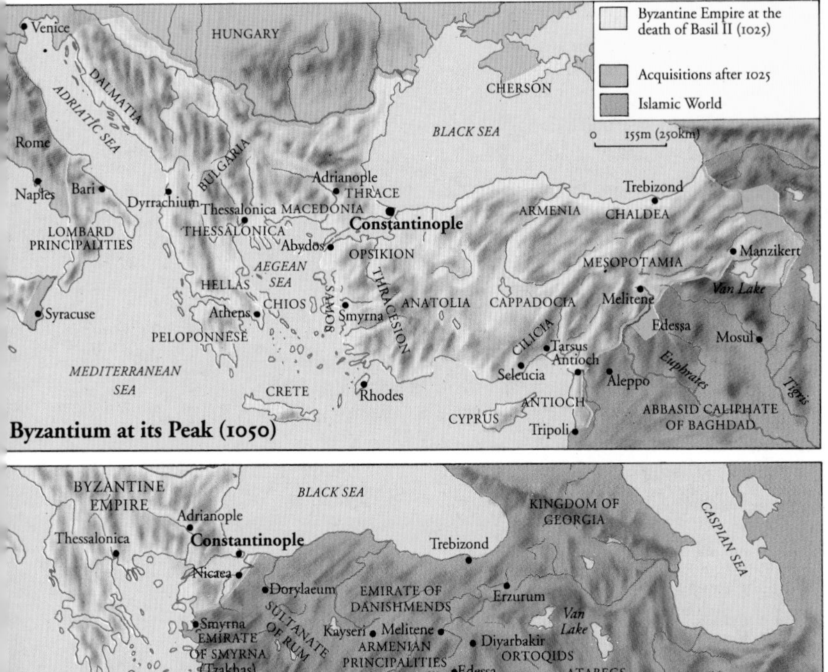

The accession of Alexius I Comnenus to the throne in 1081 (opposite) signaled the political victory of the military; his successes, however, were compromised by the commercial privileges granted to the Venetians in exchange for their naval support.

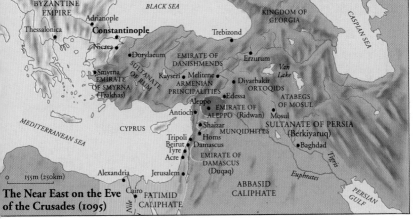

After the year 1000 the large-scale invasions ceased and the population slowly began to expand. The peasants, armed now with better tools, cleared and enlarged the small parcels of land that they had reclaimed from the forest, and agricultural production increased. Using more productive farming methods, farmers created a surplus, which in turn encouraged trade. A steady and more abundant food source made famines and epidemics less frequent and severe. Cities began to grow and set themselves off from the country. Even so, they could not compare to the rich metropolises of the East (the most populous among the western cities boasted no more than ten thousand inhabitants).

Westerners began making long voyages again, following the northern routes through Scandinavia and the Russian plains, crossing Central Europe and following the Danube River, and sailing the Mediterranean Sea from Italy and Catalonia. They exported raw materials and slaves and imported luxury goods. They could be found in the eastern ports, in Constantinople, along the Syrian coast, and in Alexandria.

The Emergence of Chivalry

During the years of invasions, the nobility had undertaken the defense of their own lands. In theory, they represented the king, who had invested them with the "right to keep order" in his name—to govern, to judge, and to punish. But in fact, from the refuges of their wooden castles, they ruled their districts with heavy hands, intent mostly on defending their possessions, which increased as more and more people came to them for protection. With the agricultural boom of the 11th century, the value of the lords' lands increased and they could now afford greater luxuries, which in turn encouraged the development of industry and the arts.

The art of warfare was changing as well. Clad in armor and helmets, the lords perfected their defensive and offensive arms. War became the domain of specialists. A future warrior had to be trained from birth, and his family had to be wealthy to pay for the necessary equipment—most importantly, a horse. The peasants were thus relegated to labor, a division that lasted for many centuries.

In the course of the 11th century these lords and their

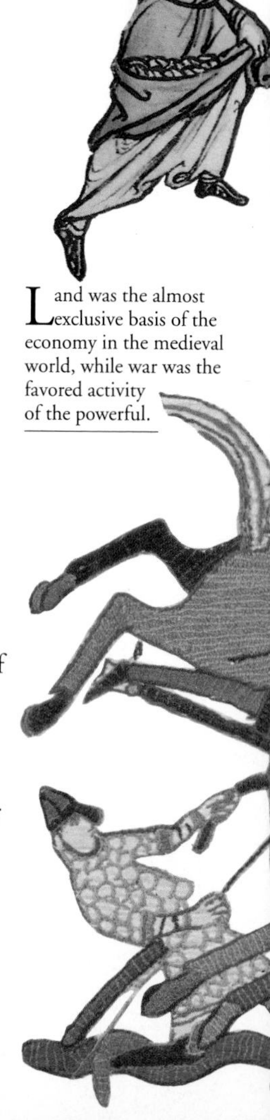

Land was the almost exclusive basis of the economy in the medieval world, while war was the favored activity of the powerful.

companions came to be called *milites.* Although this term originally referred to foot soldiers, it now signified an elite class of mounted knights. At the top of the social hierarchy, the *milites* were set apart from other men through their privileges, their behavior, and their attitudes. They formed a society of males that excluded women. They valued courage and strength, choosing to remain illiterate, for the education of the mind diminished their strength. They pledged themselves to loyalty and honor as well as courage. They fought in large units, called *batailles,* or battalions. Their preferred military tactic was the furious charge with lowered lances, an approach calculated to scatter the infantry, but which required large, open terrain.

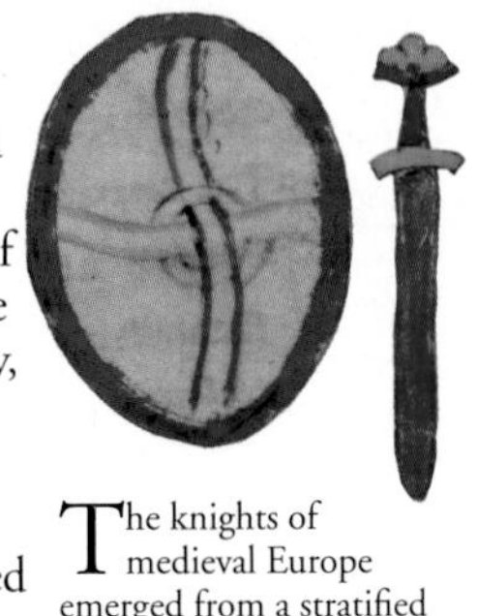

The knights of medieval Europe emerged from a stratified society. The most powerful lords had usurped the public powers in the name of the emperor. Then the crumbling political situation led to the emergence, beginning in northern France, of "lesser" lords, who ruled over very small rural districts. At the bottom of the ladder were the "landed" gentry, whose rights had been reduced to those of landowner over the peasants. Private wars between feuding lords had become a way of life.

The Church Transformed the Knights into Soldiers of God

The Church tried to contain the constant skirmishes between rival lords that had become so much a part of feudal society and had resulted in this elite class of knights. It instituted, among other measures, "the Peace of God," which forbade violence during holy periods. But the knights, fighting for the honor of their lords, had become such a strong force that the Church could not entirely dismiss what they stood for. The knights, too, wanted the Church's backing in their valiant endeavors. These two seemingly irreconcilable elements of feudal society formed an unlikely partnership during the crusades. With the support of the Church the knight became a pious hero charged with protecting the persons and the property of the Church, as well as the weak, the poor, the widows, and the orphans—all in the name of God. His supreme task was now the struggle against the "infidel."

In the 11th century monks played a decisive role in the reformation of society. They supported the popes' efforts to remove the clergy from feudal influence. Urban II (opposite above), elected pope in 1088, wanted to impose a full reform program to change the corrupt behavior of the clergy, limit the increasing power of laymen in the Church, and encroach on the absolute power of the Germanic emperors.

Reform in the Church

The Church was also experiencing renewed vigor after long-needed reforms. A religious fervor among Church followers, who were making pilgrimages and joining monasteries in larger numbers than ever before, had led to the creation of several new monastic orders. The most famous among them, the order of Cluny, became the model for monasteries across Europe. Founded in 910, it boosted the vitality of the Church with its beautiful buildings and elaborate ceremonies. By the beginning of the 11th century, however, there was a growing feeling among clergy and laypeople alike that the Cluniacs had become too attached to their material possessions and lavish rituals. Reformers favored a more disciplined monastic lifestyle; consequently, ascetic orders like the Cistercians and the even more austere Carthusians were formed.

Towards the end of the century the balance of power in the Mediterranean had begun to shift in favor of the West. Spain, which had been conquered by the Muslims, was being slowly won back; while the Seljuk threat had seemed a fierce one, the sultans had not been able to unify after the death of Malik Shah; and Byzantium had lost a huge chunk of its empire. At last it looked as though the West had an advantage. Pope Urban II wisely seized the day and made his move, rousing all Christians for a great expedition to establish sovereignty over the Holy Land.

Now "soldiers of Christ," knights supplied with powerful horses adopted a new way of fighting: The lance ceased to be a missile and became a weapon of impact, as can be seen in the training joust pictured below, where the lances have been equipped with protective balls at their ends.

Holy War, Pilgrimage, and Crusade

As the place where Christ lived, died, and was resurrected, Palestine—and particularly Jerusalem—held a special importance for Christians. Further, in the eyes of the Church, a pilgrimage to the Holy Land would bring about the forgiveness of one's sins. This belief was associated with a group of images that linked heavenly Jerusalem and earthly Jerusalem, among others. At the end of time, heavenly Jerusalem would descend and replace earthly Jerusalem. Dying in the Holy Land thus allowed one to be close to Christ at the Last Judgment. The pilgrimage to Jerusalem, facilitated by the creation of hospices—lodgings maintained by religious orders along pilgrim routes—had taken on the shape of a massive collective enterprise: In 1064–5, close to twelve thousand people were sent to the Holy Land by Gunther, bishop of Bamberg.

At the beginning of the 11th century the voyage became more perilous. The Fatimid caliph al-Hakim persecuted the Christian pilgrims and the Turkish conquests created new difficulties, interrupting the pilgrimage to the Holy Land. The pope's goal, therefore, was to reestablish free access to the Holy Land.

When he called for a crusade at the Council of Clermont in 1095, Pope Urban II also had political considerations in mind. The news from the East, which confirmed the appeal for help by the Byzantine emperor, Alexius, indicated that the eastern bastion of Christianity was in great danger. On the other hand, there was no better way for the pope to gather the various and turbulent elements of the Christian West together under his cloak than to engage them in this immense and audacious enterprise of conquering the Holy Land. While religious motives were

Theologians of the Middle Ages predicted the end of time would take place in Jerusalem, the "navel of the world." Pilgrimage to Jerusalem went back to the 4th century, after Emperor Constantine's mother, Helena, believed she had discovered there the "True Cross" and the site of the Crucifixion. The map of Jerusalem shown below, idealized into the perfect form of the circle, indicates the major monuments and sanctuaries of the city. Opposite below: A crusader, perhaps King Henry III of England, offers his services to God and the crusades.

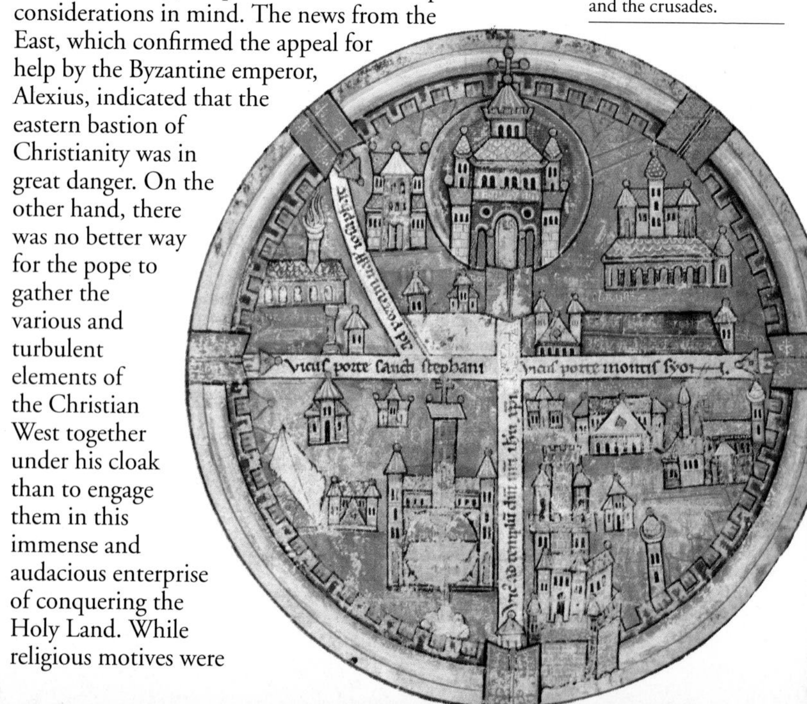

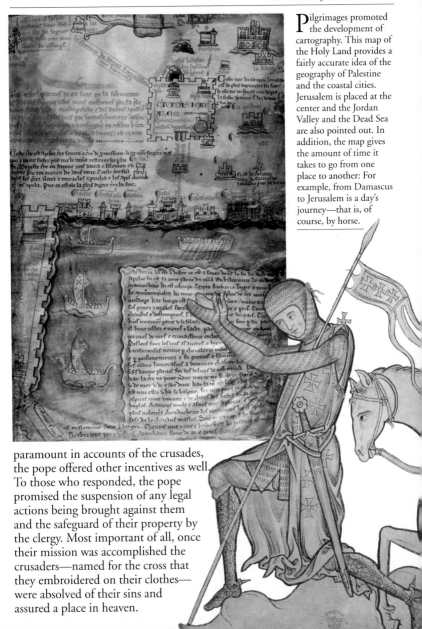

Pilgrimages promoted the development of cartography. This map of the Holy Land provides a fairly accurate idea of the geography of Palestine and the coastal cities. Jerusalem is placed at the center and the Jordan Valley and the Dead Sea are also pointed out. In addition, the map gives the amount of time it takes to go from one place to another: For example, from Damascus to Jerusalem is a day's journey—that is, of course, by horse.

paramount in accounts of the crusades, the pope offered other incentives as well. To those who responded, the pope promised the suspension of any legal actions being brought against them and the safeguard of their property by the clergy. Most important of all, once their mission was accomplished the crusaders—named for the cross that they embroidered on their clothes—were absolved of their sins and assured a place in heaven.

et aultres sains lieux la environ.
Et les xpiens pabitans & demou
rans. & que les aultres par eulx
tyrannicquement & inhumaine
ment tuez. Ilz avoient reservez
en infelicieuse vie afin que sur
eulx en lopprobre du saint nom
xpien peussent continuer plus
longuement leurs insatiables
cruaultez. Et comment ilz
les tenoient en trop opprobrieuse
captivite & servaige. ou tresgrant
deshonneur & opprobre de tous
les xpiens. Concluant & mon
strant par diverses raisons tres
evidentes que le saint peuple
xpien ne debvoit plus souffrir
ne endurer que les sains lieux et

The goal of the First Crusade and the mass of men it set in motion caught Byzantium and the Islamic world by surprise. It resulted in the creation of western settlements—or Latin states, as they became known—in the East. Until 1130 the West had the upper hand. The Franks—as the western invaders were called—established large settlements and built mighty "crusader castles" to guard them. But the Muslims managed to block their advance and bring about a reversal in the balance of power.

CHAPTER II
THE FIRST CRUSADE

Urban II kept his plan for a crusade a secret until the last moment. The first nine days of the Council of Clermont (opposite) were devoted to issues of discipline. On 27 November 1095 the pope startled everyone with his appeal to Christians to rescue the Holy Land.

Peter the Hermit began his fervent preaching in the Berri in central France and continued it through the regions of Orléanais, Champagne, Lorraine, and western Germany. From the beginning his image was distorted by legend. It was said that during a pilgrimage to the church of the Holy Sepulcher (opposite below), Christ directed him to go to the pope and aid him in preaching the crusade. Some fifteen thousand people accompanied him from France (left). Unfortunately, this mass turned out to be unruly; on their way out of Hungary, the pilgrims took Zemun (present-day Semlin) and killed four thousand Hungarians. On gaining the Byzantine Empire, they pillaged Belgrade and then sacked the towns around Nish. In desperation the Byzantine emperor imposed restrictions on them and said he would continue to feed them only if they stayed no longer than three days in any town. Above: Cross from the First Crusade.

Pope Urban II's Appeal Mobilized Knights and Poor Men

The reception given his proposal to go forth and conquer the Holy Land surprised the pope. He knew he could count on the knights of southern France, where he had first made his appeal, in particular on Raymond of Saint-Gilles, count of Toulouse. Raymond was an extremely wealthy lord, and his retinue alone—which included his wife—made up a good-size troop. But three other armies of knights came to join this one: Under Godfrey of Bouillon were the northern French, Lorrainers, and Germans; lords from the Ile-de-France (the region around Paris) and Champagne led by Hugh of Vermandois, brother to the king of France; and, finally, Normans from southern Italy and Sicily under the leadership of Bohemond of Taranto and his nephew Tancred. Made up of knights, these four armies did not belong to any particular kingdom, but the most powerful among the volunteers, no doubt, had dreams of becoming rulers of their own little principalities in the East.

The pope had aimed his appeal at the *milites,* whose fighting skills would be essential to the success of the expedition. But to his enormous surprise, hordes of common people thronged the roads after the harvest in August 1096 to join the crusade. Gripped by religious fervor, the poor of all walks of life "took the cross," alone or with their families and their portable goods, forming a veritable migration. By killing the infidels and going to die in earthly Jerusalem, they believed they would be present at the Day of Judgment, when heavenly Jerusalem, with its "walls of jasper and gates of pearls," would descend to Earth. Peter the Hermit, a preacher, placed himself at the head of this mass—the People's Crusade—ultimately overshadowing the role of the pope.

Godfrey of Bouillon (left, leaving for the crusade) did not play a leading role until the attack on Jerusalem on 15 July 1099: At the head of the crusaders from Lorraine, at the northeast section of the ramparts, he was one of the first to invade the city, using the wooden tower he had built. He was elected the first ruler of the kingdom of Jerusalem. Renowned for his strength, courage, and straightforward behavior, he soon became a mythical figure and was known as the Knight of the Swan.

The People's Crusade Reached Constantinople in the Autumn of 1096

The long march of the crusaders was marked by carnage, pillage, and destruction: the massacre of Jews in the Rhineland; thieving and slaughter in Hungary and the Byzantine Empire. The havoc wrought by these large masses of poor people, who had to be fed in order to prevent their depredations, greatly alarmed the Byzantines, and

Tancred was Bohemond's nephew and loyal lieutenant. He captured Tarsus (left, he receives the key of the city) and Adana. He was the first to hoist his standard onto the walls of Jerusalem, where he tried, unsuccessfully, to protect Muslim prisoners from being massacred. Tancred conquered the kingdom of Galilee but maintained chivalric relations with some Arab leaders. Yet he always remained hostile to the Byzantines.

all those in their path, and presented insoluble problems. Instead of the trained soldiers-for-hire that the Byzantine Emperor Alexius had envisioned to help back up his own troops in their fight against the Muslims, he found himself with a hungry, untrained mass of German and French peasants at his doorstep. At their request (and to his relief), Alexius had the crusaders transported to the opposite shores of the Bosporus. They headed for Turkish territory, where they suffered two terrible defeats. The emperor then organized the return of the survivors to Europe. Their defeat, however, served to bolster the mistrust of the Western Christians—or Franks—toward the Eastern Christians—the Byzantines, or Greeks, as they were also called—who came to be viewed as heretics, degenerates, and traitors. Likewise, the savage behavior of the crusaders filled the Byzantines with horror—and regret.

Below: The massacre of the inhabitants of Antioch.

The Lords Swore Fealty to the Byzantine Emperor

The lords arrived next in Constantinople—still no sign of the mercenaries that Alexius had requested. The emperor again had to protect himself from the crusaders' violations of his own empire's security, while at the same time deploying them against his enemies, the Turks. After much insisting he succeeded in having the lords swear an oath of loyalty to him; they agreed to return to him (rather than keep for themselves) all the territory that had belonged to the Byzantine Empire before the Turkish conquest and to recognize his sovereignty over other lands that they might conquer in the East.

After crossing Anatolia, suffering greatly from hunger and thirst, the crusaders arrived in Cilicia, at the doors of Syria, where they were welcomed by the Christian Armenians who had lived there since the mid-11th

century. From there the crusaders split up; some wanted to carve out their own principalities, while others, including the members of the People's Crusade, remained loyal to their religious objectives.

The people of Antioch held off Bohemond and the crusaders for eight months (above). Short on provisions the crusaders had to trek almost sixty miles away from the city, across dangerous terrain, for food. In May 1098 their situation took a desperate turn: A large army led by Kerboga, *atabeg* of Mosul, was said to be on its way. Bohemond, helped by a Christian Armenian within the city walls, saved the day by capturing the city two days before Kerboga's arrival.

Baldwin, Brother of Godfrey of Bouillon, Founded the County of Edessa

The region of the Taurus Mountains was filled with Christian sects like the Jacobite Syrians and Armenians, who hated the Greeks (by whom they had been kicked out of Armenia) as much as, if not more than, the Muslims. They greeted the Franks as liberators. Thoros, the Armenian prince of Edessa, who did not have the might to withstand a Turkish attack on his own, appealed to the crusader Baldwin of Boulogne for help. Having no children himself Thoros adopted Baldwin as his son, making him both heir and joint ruler. However, a Greek Orthodox by religion, Thoros's standing among his people was always precarious, and he was killed during an uprising (perhaps instigated by his new heir). As his successor, Baldwin proclaimed himself count of Edessa in March 1098, founding the first crusader state.

The besiegers became the besieged, as the starving Franks awaited Kerboga's arrival. A well-timed miracle lifted the crusaders' spirits: Peter Bartholomew, a cleric, had a revelation concerning the place where the lance that had pierced Christ's side was buried. A lance was indeed found buried where he indicated. The crusaders' zeal reached such a pitch that they launched an attack and dispersed Kerboga's army on 28 June 1098. From left to right: The crusaders before Antioch; the attack on and capture of the city; and the surrender and the entry of the crusaders in Antioch. The massacre of the inhabitants is pictured below.

The Siege of Antioch Lasted from October 1097 to June 1098

The crusaders reached the gates of Antioch on 20 October 1097. Retaken by the Byzantines in 960 and back in Muslim hands by 1085, the city had lost the magnificence it had enjoyed in its Roman days. Still, it

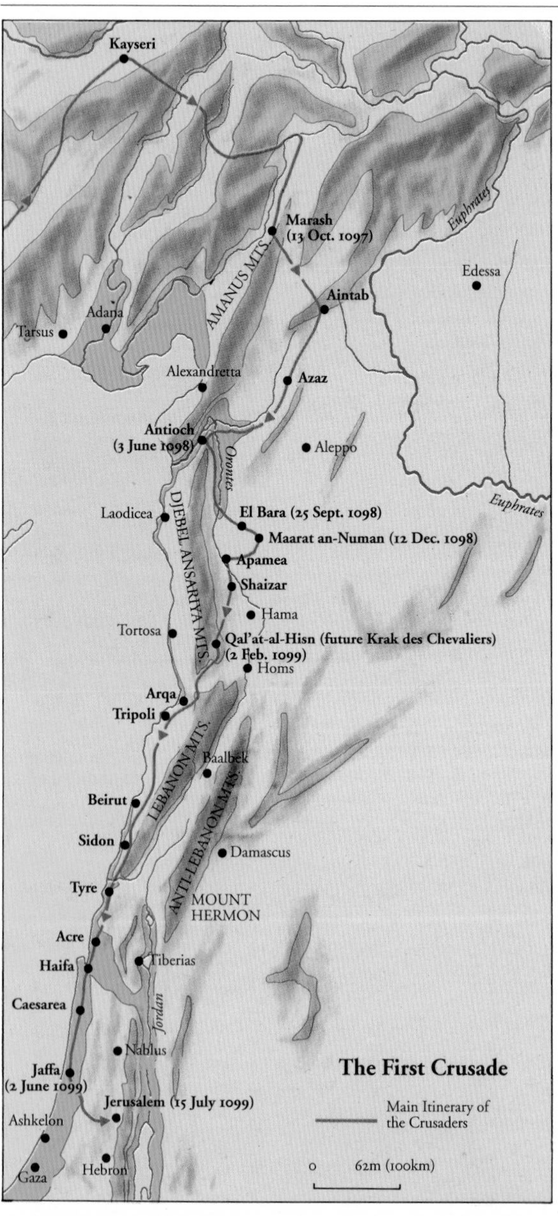

The crusaders left Europe in 1096 and did not reach Jerusalem until three years later. The passage through Anatolia was particularly difficult. The Franks preferred the direct route through its center to the longer route along the coast. On 19 June 1097 they took Nicaea, at the entrance to Asia Minor. Kilij Arslan and the Danishmends joined forces against them but were defeated at the large-scale battle of Dorylaeum on 1 July 1097: The route to Anatolia was now open. The Franks crossed vast desert tracts. After taking Iconium (present-day Konya), they arrived at Heraclea, at the foot of the Taurus Mountains. From there the crusaders split into two groups. A small troop, led by Baldwin, crossed the Taurus and captured Cilicia. For unknown reasons the bulk of the troop made a circle around Anatolia, to Caesarea, before coming down to Antioch. This detour gave them the chance to repel the rest of the Turkish forces. After the siege of Antioch, which lasted seven months, they moved inland, going through Maarat an-Numan. They then swerved towards the coast, which they followed to Palestine, arriving at Jerusalem on 7 June 1099.

was a fortress unlike any the crusaders had ever seen (most of the castles in the West were still made of wood). Its six-mile-long wall was guarded by 450 towers and a citadel rising more than one thousand feet over the city. Lacking the proper arms, the crusaders could not storm the fortress. They received word that a large Muslim army, led by Kerboga, was on its way to help defend Antioch. Acting quickly the crusaders were able to enter the city with the help of a traitor. The army of Kerboga arrived too late and was defeated after a drawn-out siege.

To demoralize their opponents, the Franks threw at them the heads of Turks killed in combat.

The capture of Antioch was the turning point of the First Crusade and opened the road to Jerusalem. But some of the crusaders had other plans. Although they had sworn to the Byzantine emperor that all his newly freed lands would be returned to him, some of them intended to keep Antioch for themselves. Bohemond of Taranto claimed it for his role in the victory (he was the one who had convinced the traitor to sell the city). The principality of Antioch became the second crusader—or Latin—state.

While the Lords Fought Among Themselves, the Ranks Pressed On

By contrast, some of the poorer crusaders agitated to continue the expedition. They had begun believing the preachers who taught

them that destitution was a condition of salvation. Propelled by a new fervor—and hunger—they formed a troop of Tafurs, "half-civilized Flemings," who became the spearhead of the army, instilling terror among the Muslims. They had no military might—no lances or shields, only cudgels—so sure were they that Providence would provide for them. Their uncontrolled behavior scandalized the natives and even some knights: They killed the Muslims systematically and after battle sometimes even turned cannibalistic, eating the bodies of their fallen enemies.

In December 1098 the crusaders took Maarat an-Numan, in Syria's interior. In order to keep the western lords from giving free reign to their appetite for cities, lands, and goods, the Tafurs massacred the population and destroyed the town. They thus forced the lords to continue on to Jerusalem after more than a year of diversions. In the south the crusaders entered an area where the Turks were less in evidence and a multitude of Arab emirates held sway. Most of the emirs were too weak to resist the crusaders, who passed through their lands without incident. They returned to the Orontes

"The other princes, after having put to death in the various neighborhoods of the city all those they came across, having learned that a large part of the population had taken refuge behind the ramparts of the Temple, hastened there together, carrying in their wake an immense multitude of knights and foot soldiers, striking all those they met with their swords, sparing no one, and flooded the place with the blood of the infidels; in this way they carried out the just decrees of God so that those who had profaned the sanctuary of the Lord by their superstitious acts, rendering it from that time alien to the faithful, would purify it in their

turn with their own blood, and suffer death in the same place in expiation for their crimes. One could not, nonetheless, look on that multitude of corpses without horror, scattered arms and legs heaped on the floor on all sides, and streams of blood flooding the surface of the floor.”

The capture of Jerusalem, in *Historia Rerum*, William of Tyre, a 12th-century historian born in Jerusalem

The Franks circled Jerusalem in procession before attacking (above left to right) and massacring the inhabitants (below).

River, outside of Antioch, regained the coast, and skirted the coastal side of the Lebanon Mountains.

The Capture of Jerusalem: Fasts, Processions, Attacks, and Massacres

The crusaders who reached Jerusalem in 1099 marveled at the sight: The city sparkled in the sun. They thought they had attained the heavenly Jerusalem. All fell on their knees, wishing to carry out the will of the Creator, who would help them to break down the city's walls. The crusaders declared a public fast before the attack set for 13 June. The attack, however, failed to come off for want of ladders. Confident of a

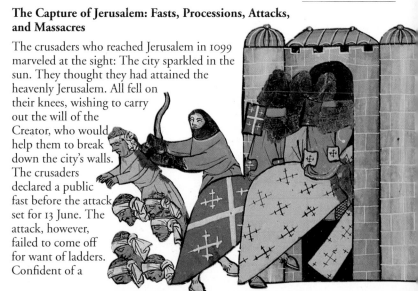

The Crusaders at the Holy Sepulcher

Although grandiose and highly stylized, this 19th-century painting and those on the following four pages capture the fervor of the Franks on reaching the city of Jerusalem. They omit, however, the denouement: Without the arrival of a Genoese fleet at Jaffa, the Franks would not have succeeded in capturing Jerusalem. The first painting (left) shows Peter the Hermit, leader of the "People's Crusade" and one of the preachers who stirred up the masses as the procession was circling the city. The second (overleaf) evokes the Franks' excitement on capturing the city. In the background is the Dome of the Rock, or the mosque of Umar, built on the place from which Muhammad is said to have ascended to heaven. The third painting (pages 50–1) represents the crusaders at the church of the Holy Sepulcher, known as the church of the Resurrection, where they sang a hymn of triumph and gratitude.

"When they deemed that the Savior had been sufficiently avenged, that is, when hardly anyone in the city was left alive, they all went to worship at the holy tomb with tears, groans, and the beating of chests."

Jules Michelet

miracle, the crusaders had not come prepared with any equipment necessary for a siege and soon became the besieged, as they had no water, provisions, equipment, or skilled craftsmen to build the equipment.

Just in time a fleet of six Genoese and four English ships put in at Jaffa, north of Jerusalem. They brought with them wood and carpenters. Reduced to twelve thousand men, starved and hemmed in, the crusaders presented a sorry sight. They declared another public fast and on 8 July circled the city in a barefoot procession led by the clergy—Israel surrounding the walls of Jericho—but these walls remained upright. On 10 July 1099 they attacked; five days later they scaled the walls and took the city. Jews and Muslims alike came under their swords or were burned (the Christians who lived there had already been expelled by the Fatimid governor). For two days the crusaders did nothing but kill and pillage. The few surviving Jews were sold into slavery, and a small number of Muslims were able to seek refuge in Damascus. Such barbarous and savage behavior shocked the entire Middle East and made an impression that would never be forgotten.

It was religious feeling rather than political considerations that led Godfrey to choose for his title not king but "defender of the Holy Sepulcher," where he went to pray as soon as the city was captured.

Godfrey of Bouillon, Defender of the Holy Sepulcher

After the capture of Jerusalem the victors—an army of the poor, lords, and clergy alike—agreed the city should be kept and defended. Yet they could not concur on a form of government for the new kingdom. The poor and the clergy argued for a theocracy rather than a monarchy, because they felt it was inappropriate for a king to rule in the place where the Savior had been crucified; a defender sufficed. The clergy thought the crusade should result in the establishment of a true Christian kingdom, a pontifical state governed by the successor to Saint Peter. Since the pope could not assume this power in person, it should be conferred on his legates, in the person of Daimbert, bishop of Pisa.

The lords felt differently. They were not about to let the reins of the Holy Land escape them. Soon after the capture of Jerusalem they convened to choose a leader. The only two contenders were Godfrey of Bouillon and Raymond of Saint-Gilles. The former was chosen, a respected knight with a mild manner who would give little offense to the other knights. Refusing the title of king, he dubbed himself "defender of the Holy Sepulcher." Known for his courage and piety, Godfrey was said to be so devout that his family was often forced to eat cold, overcooked meals while they waited for him to return from prayers. Daimbert was later elected patriarch of Jerusalem. On his deathbed Godfrey nominated his brother Baldwin, count of Edessa, to succeed him.

Taken from a 12th-century manuscript, this map of Jerusalem is relatively accurate. It shows the Holy Sepulcher, the Tower of David, and numerous sanctuaries.

The sculpture below commemorates a returning crusader being welcomed by his wife. He wears the symbols of a pilgrim: the purse (or scrip), the staff, and the cross.

The Founding of the Kingdom of Jerusalem

Baldwin I was less self-effacing than his brother and had himself crowned king of Bethlehem. While a monarchy was created in Jerusalem, there was little kingdom for it to rule. The Franks controlled only a slender piece of land. Most of the crusaders, having delivered on their promise to rescue Jerusalem, returned home. Baldwin had only about two hundred knights and one thousand soldiers under his command. A new threat, the Egyptians, was drawing near.

The call for crusaders did not stop, and three large

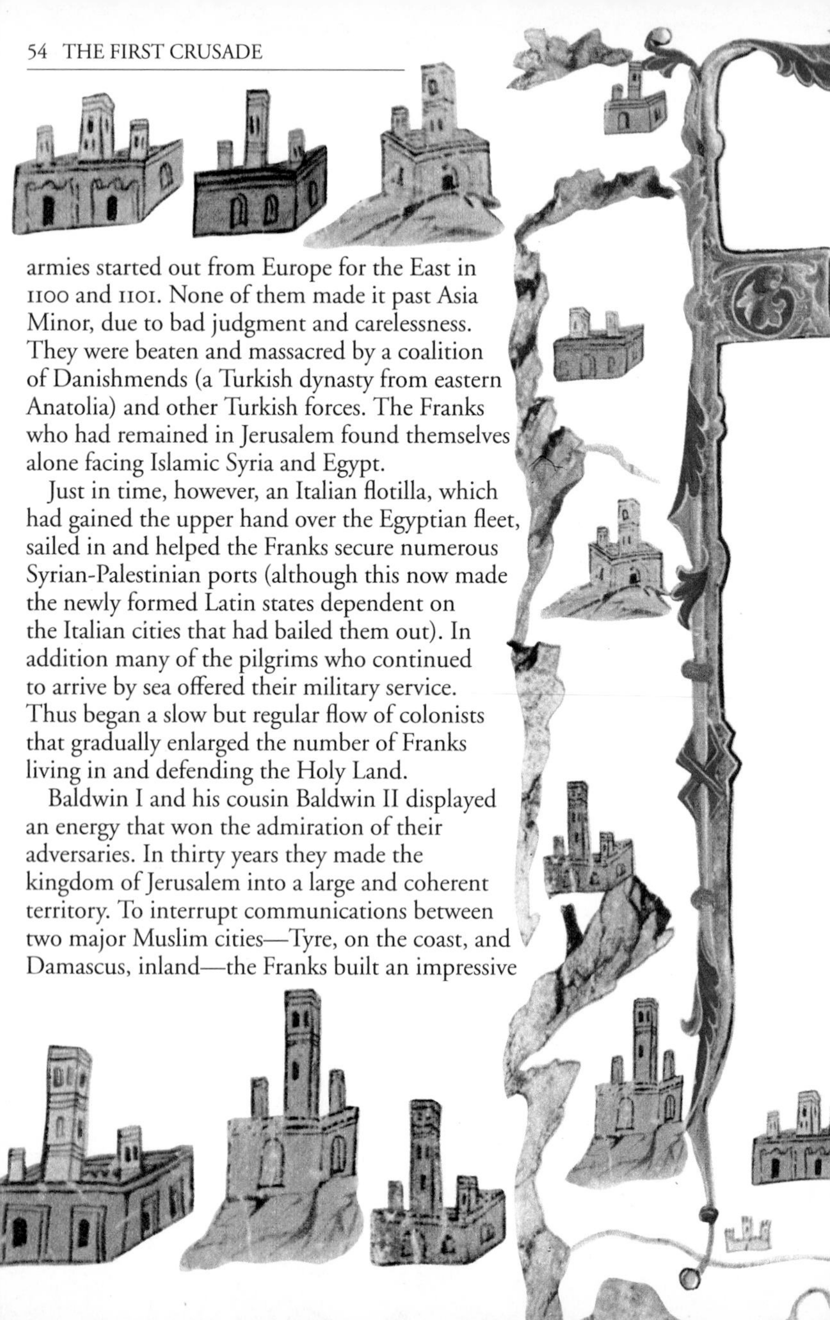

armies started out from Europe for the East in 1100 and 1101. None of them made it past Asia Minor, due to bad judgment and carelessness. They were beaten and massacred by a coalition of Danishmends (a Turkish dynasty from eastern Anatolia) and other Turkish forces. The Franks who had remained in Jerusalem found themselves alone facing Islamic Syria and Egypt.

Just in time, however, an Italian flotilla, which had gained the upper hand over the Egyptian fleet, sailed in and helped the Franks secure numerous Syrian-Palestinian ports (although this now made the newly formed Latin states dependent on the Italian cities that had bailed them out). In addition many of the pilgrims who continued to arrive by sea offered their military service. Thus began a slow but regular flow of colonists that gradually enlarged the number of Franks living in and defending the Holy Land.

Baldwin I and his cousin Baldwin II displayed an energy that won the admiration of their adversaries. In thirty years they made the kingdom of Jerusalem into a large and coherent territory. To interrupt communications between two major Muslim cities—Tyre, on the coast, and Damascus, inland—the Franks built an impressive

network of fortresses and castles (called "kraks," after the Arabic word for castle) and tried to take Banias, a town at the foot of Mount Hermon that controlled the road to Damascus. They hoped to capture Damascus itself, but failing this, concluded a treaty with Damascus, agreeing to share between them the revenues of Bekaa and Gilead. Crusaders settled in Idumaea and Moab, where they took possession of the castle of Montreal, fifty miles from Aqaba. From there they could keep an eye on the movements between Egypt and Syria, as well as raid caravans and rob Muslim pilgrims heading for Mecca. In addition they forced the Bedouins of Arabia to pay them an annual tribute.

The Northern States Expanded While the County of Tripoli Formed Slowly

The county of Edessa, which had a Christian Armenian majority, soon reached its full dimensions. The principality of Antioch faced the emirate of Aleppo to its east and Byzantium to its north, which made attempts to retake the area. The princes of Antioch repulsed the Byzantines and established themselves from beyond the Orontes to Apamea; at Al-Bara they installed the first Catholic bishop —in a direct affront to the Byzantine Church. Eventually they subdued the emir of Aleppo and made a treaty with him.

Bertrand of Saint-Gilles, count of Tripoli, did not take his city—the fourth Latin state—until 1109. His county was bordered on the east by the Ansariya and Lebanon mountains, which were held by

The Syrian-Palestinian coast is endowed with a double line of parallel and almost continuous mountain ranges, which break off only when they reach Antioch and Homs. From north to south, they start with the Amanus (Nur) chain, the Djebel Ansariya, and then the Lebanon Mountains. The mountains to the east are lower except at the point behind the Lebanon Mountains, where the Anti-Lebanon chain, including Mount Hermon, sits not two miles away. These regions provided refuge for various minorities: the Ismailis in the Ansariya Mountains; and the Maronites, Shias, and Druzes in Mount Lebanon. The fiercely independent nature of these sects made the mountains more than just physically daunting. The Franks built many castles (as seen on this map of the Holy Land), from which they could both keep an eye on the native populations and control the trade and pilgrim routes.

the Assassins and the Maronites—a persecuted offshoot of the Syrian Church, who earned a reputation as a hardy and warlike people. While the mountains provided a protective barrier, the area was exposed at the Homs Pass. In 1110 the Franks took two fortresses, which they never stopped repairing and enlarging: the Chastel Blanc and the great Krak des Chevaliers, which watched over the northeast side of Tripoli.

The Franks Maintained A United Front

Despite many disagreements the Franks benefited from a true sense of unity. The authority of the king of Jerusalem gradually grew stronger. The political stability of the Frankish states was such that even the imprisonment of King Baldwin II between 1123 and 1125 by the Turks did not impair it.

Another strength was the effectiveness of the Frankish army. The imposing western knights, covered entirely in armor and mounted on sturdy horses, were overpowering in attack. However, the Franks were a minority and their army, though superior under certain conditions, lost its advantage on rough terrain. With their more agile cavalry and deadly weapons, the Turkish and Arab forces gained the upper hand when they could use surprise tactics.

The cavalry was of no help whatsoever while laying siege, but certain weapons did prove useful. The "quarrelers" and "mangonels" hurled stones and arrows against the ramparts. The catapults launched steel hooks attached to ropes that shook the walls when the ropes were pulled. The "battering rams," shielded beneath wooden structures, pounded the ramparts with enormous beams covered with iron heads. The most useful weapon was the siege "engine." A movable wooden tower several stories high, it rose above the walls of the besieged city. Beneath, it enclosed a battering ram; the intermediate stories carried longbowmen and crossbowmen; at the top level, a footbridge could be lowered onto the wall.

Muslim Forces Regrouped

From the first, the Muslim states resisted the settlement of the Franks. After the First Crusade, they regrouped. In 1101 they devastated the second wave of crusaders in Asia Minor. From that time until 1130 they led periodic attacks, many of which came close to succeeding. Between 1101 and 1105 the Fatimids carried out five offensives on land. Each of these expeditions placed the Franks at mortal risk,

Mobile towers were generally covered with animal skins soaked in vinegar to protect them from the flaming clay pots hurled by the city defenders.

tying up the Frankish forces for weeks and entailing great expenditures. What saved them was the breach between the two Muslim powers—Egypt and Damascus.

However, between 1105 and 1108 Egypt and Damascus established an alliance. The crusaders' conquest of the important port city of Acre was a deciding factor. The alliance was not very effective since the Egyptians, who were maintaining by sea the coastal cities that had not yet fallen, were soon overpowered by the Italian flotillas, then at the height of their strength. Without maritime support the Egyptians could not attack with full force.

The Franks sought to terrorize the besieged by showing them the heads severed from their fellow Muslims. Such ploys were not nearly as effective as the famine brought on by a prolonged siege or a direct attack, with all its dangers.

The Strongest Muslim Resistance Came from Northern Syria

The crusaders grew ever more numerous and their attacks more frequent. The emirate of Aleppo was vulnerable on all sides. When Egypt and Damascus could spare no more troops, the emir appealed to Baghdad for help. The Franks failed in their attempt on Mosul, an important town on the caravan route to Baghdad. In 1104 they suffered a stinging defeat at Harran, another trading center. In 1110 the Seljuk sultan commanded the emir of Mosul, Mawdud, who was from the clan of the Ortoqid (a Turkish tribal group), to assemble a coalition of Muslims to attack the Franks. This united front began its attack on the county of Edessa. The Franks made the astounding decision to evacuate all of the civilians living in the

The Turkish cavalry (left and opposite right) did not seek direct confrontations; instead it surrounded the small Frankish armies and showered them with arrows in order to break them up into groups. The Franks unified against this tactic only at the battle of Arsuf in 1191.

fortified settlement to the other side of the Euphrates. The Franks then crossed back over the river to defend the stronghold. The Turks, who were already in the vicinity, seized the opportunity and butchered the civilians —while the Franks watched helplessly from across the river. Although he did not capture the capital, Mawdud inflicted on the

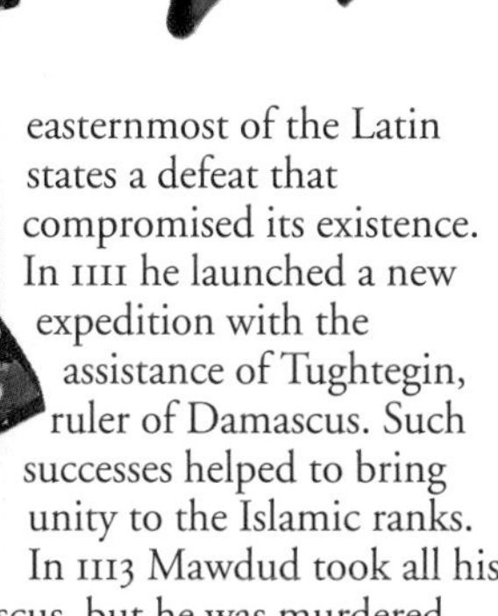

easternmost of the Latin states a defeat that compromised its existence. In 1111 he launched a new expedition with the assistance of Tughtegin, ruler of Damascus. Such successes helped to bring unity to the Islamic ranks. In 1113 Mawdud took all his troops with him to Damascus, but he was murdered there by a member of the fierce sect of Assassins.

"Ager Sanguinis," the Blood-Stained Muslim Victory

The central location of Aleppo, in northern Syria, had made it a major player in the struggle for supremacy in the region. It was fought over by the Franks as well as various Muslim factions. Roger of Antioch led repeated attacks against the kingdom until finally the people of Aleppo turned to the Muslim leader Ilghazi for help. He dealt Roger a stunning blow in 1119, on a battlefield halfway between Aleppo and Antioch that came to be called by the Franks "Ager Sanguinis," or "Field of Blood." The Frankish army was decimated, Roger of

"God gave victory to the Muslims. The Franks who fled back to their camp were massacred and from all sides the Turks charged, as though a single man; arrows flew through the air like a swarm of locusts; under the shower of shafts, which struck the cavalry and the main body of the army, the Franks beat a hasty retreat. After the defeat of the cavalry and the annihilation of the infantry, the valets and pages were all taken prisoners. Sire Roger was killed. The Muslims only lost twenty men; by contrast there were only about twenty Franks who survived. One of their leaders was among these survivors, but close to fifteen thousand men remained dead on the ground.... Word of the victory reached Aleppo before the Muslims made their noonday prayer."

The battle of "Ager Sanguinis," in *Chronicle of Aleppo*, Kamal ad-Din, a 13th-century Arab historian

Salerno was killed, and prisoners who escaped death on the spot were set upon by the crowds.

Clearly it was not through lack of activity or energy that the Muslim emirs and *atabegs* failed to expel the enemy. However, despite attempts at unification, they could not maintain internal order and, most importantly, they did not follow through on their

These armaments (opposite), found at Aleppo, are classic impact weapons of the Muslims.

victories. Thus, while Mawdud massacred the people of Edessa, he did not actually take the city, and, at the pinnacle of his power, he was murdered by a fellow Muslim in Damascus. Likewise, after his great success at the "Field of Blood," Ilghazi made no further attacks, and Baldwin II was able to push him back. Still, a powerful warning had been sent to the Franks.

After the death of Ilghazi his nephew Balak took over the fight against the Franks and quickly became a hero of the Arabs. Starting in 1122 he took prisoner first Joscelin, count of Edessa, then Baldwin II, king of Jerusalem, depriving two Latin states of their rulers. He next undertook the reconquest of lands taken by the Franks surrounding Aleppo. But as he went to the aid of Tyre, which was being attacked by a Frankish-Venetian coalition, he was killed. Disheartened by his death, the Tyrians surrendered, while Ilghazi's son abandoned Aleppo and released Baldwin, who hastened to set siege to the city. The courage of the local ruler, Ibn al-Khachab, saved Aleppo, but he was stabbed by a member of the Assassins in 1125. This ever more powerful sect was preying on the world of Islam, which needed all its strength to confront its opponent.

In the representation at left, Franks and Turks are shown with the same armaments; the horses of both sides are outfitted with ostentatious trappings. Despite the lack of realism the Turks can be recognized by their headbands, as well as their lack of armor and bare legs and feet. At the battle of "Ager Sanguinis," or "Field of Blood," the Frankish army had seven hundred cavalry and three thousand foot soldiers. To these could be added the local auxiliaries: Eastern Christians, Jacobite Syrians, and Armenians. But there were few of them, and the Franks felt their loyalty could never be counted on.

With Muslim Syria divided among its many factions, the four Latin states—Jerusalem, Antioch, Edessa, and Tripoli—formed a powerful, if fragile, coalition. Their strength came from the solidity of their political institutions, which conferred a large measure of authority on the king or prince.

CHAPTER III
THE LATIN STATES OF THE EAST

Fulk, count of Anjou, one of the most powerful lords of the West, became king of Jerusalem (right). His reign, from 1131 to 1143, was marked by prosperity. He oversaw the building of fortifications throughout the kingdom. Opposite: Fresco of a praying crusader.

The King's Absolute Authority

In the kingdom of Jerusalem, as in the principality of Antioch and the county of Tripoli, the monarchy was hereditary. The nobles reserved the right to elect, that is, to confirm, the closest relative of the preceding king, but that was only a formality.

Unlike the Byzantine emperor or the caliphs of Baghdad and Cairo, the king did not rely on a complex administrative machinery. The political life of the kingdom took place in the *curia regis*, the court of the king, or the high court. All the king's vassals could participate, but it became the province of the most powerful lords and, of course, the king above all. The high court judged conflicts and confirmed the concession of fiefdoms, as well as their transmission, purchase, and sale. At court, all of the political, financial, legislative, and judicial affairs of the kingdom came under examination and discussion.

The institutions set up in the kingdom of Jerusalem matched those of western monarchies in appearance (left, the death of Baldwin II and the crowning of Fulk I), except that the Franks constituted a minority. The constant threat of danger, from within as well as without, had a unifying effect. At the outset, Jerusalem's hereditary monarchy was much stronger than any in the West. For a long time it maintained control over its fiefdoms, whose lords owed their lands directly to the king, and over its subjects, most of whom had been conquered. Despite his absolute authority, however, the king of Jerusalem needed to consult his advisors (below).

The King and His New Kingdom of Jerusalem

The kingdom of Jerusalem was divided into seignories, which were managed by seigneurs, or lords, who answered to the king. The lord held the reins of justice, mobilized his knights for war, and collected taxes. In the

first years of the Latin states' existence, the nobles were completely dependent on the king of Jerusalem, the prince of Antioch, or the counts of Tripoli and Edessa. Only the "trading estates" partially escaped the king's authority. These were colonies founded within the cities by the Italian city-states and French and Spanish cities. Socially, their members were no different from the commoners, but their status was determined by individual treaties negotiated between the rulers of the Latin East. Since so many of the crusaders had returned home after the conquest of Jerusalem, the kings and princes were left with very little military strength. With no fleets at their command they were cut off from the Christian West; further, they could not carry out campaigns against Muslim coastal cities. Thus they were forced to rely on the naval powers of the West to help them. The Italian states were, of

Over time, the powers of the king of Jerusalem—and the prince and counts of the other states (below)—grew weaker (drawings of their royal seals, at left). From the beginning some lords had more independence than others, such as Tancred, who had conquered the kingdom of Galilee with his own soldiers. The original fiefs were passed on to their heirs, who tended to be beholden to the king for their land. By the second and third generations the lords had become part of larger families that cultivated a group of vassals loyal to them. Gradually, a native aristocratic class forced the kingdom to modify its laws of inheritance to permit the accumulation of fiefdoms.

The Armenians called on the crusaders to help them escape Turkish domination, and it was in response to their appeal that Baldwin founded the county of Edessa. But the Armenians chafed under his authoritarianism and, especially, his harshness and greed. At left, the inhabitants of Edessa pay homage to King Baldwin as they hand over their tribute.

course, willing to help—but for a price. They negotiated extremely advantageous treaties with the Frankish rulers, which included tax exemptions and other legal immunities. As a result, Pisa, Genoa, and Venice all held considerable privileges in the Latin states.

The Conquered People of the Latin States

For the Muslims the loss of Jerusalem had been a religious defeat, but not a great disaster. They assumed that, like other invaders, the Franks would either eventually move on or gradually assimilate. To the surprise of the Muslims and Eastern Christians, the Franks were not like other invaders. They sought to dominate the people they had defeated. They distinguished between victor and vanquished, Frank and non-Frank, on the basis of ethnic origin and religion. There was no solidarity between the crusaders who settled in the East and the native populations. The Franks—Roman Catholic and originally from Europe—clustered in the cities. Periodic waves of immigration increased their numbers, but they remained a minority, separated from the rest of the people by a huge rift.

Muslims made up the majority of the vanquished. While they lost their edge in the cities, where they had been massacred or chased out, they predominated in the countryside, with more Sunnis to the west and Shias to the east. The Druzes, another Islamic sect, lived between Sidon and Mount

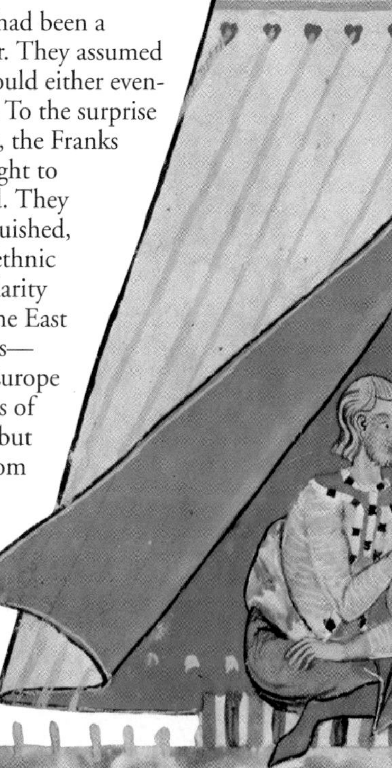

Hermon and had a reputation as formidable fighters. Replacing the Muslim landowners, the Franks subjected the peasants to certain duties. All had to pay the *jizya*, a poll tax, which under the Muslims had applied only to non-Muslims. There was also a heavy land tax, which varied depending on the type of agriculture practiced, and forced labor for the construction of buildings.

The Franks left intact the administrative machinery that was already in place in Muslim communities. Each village had a sort of mayor

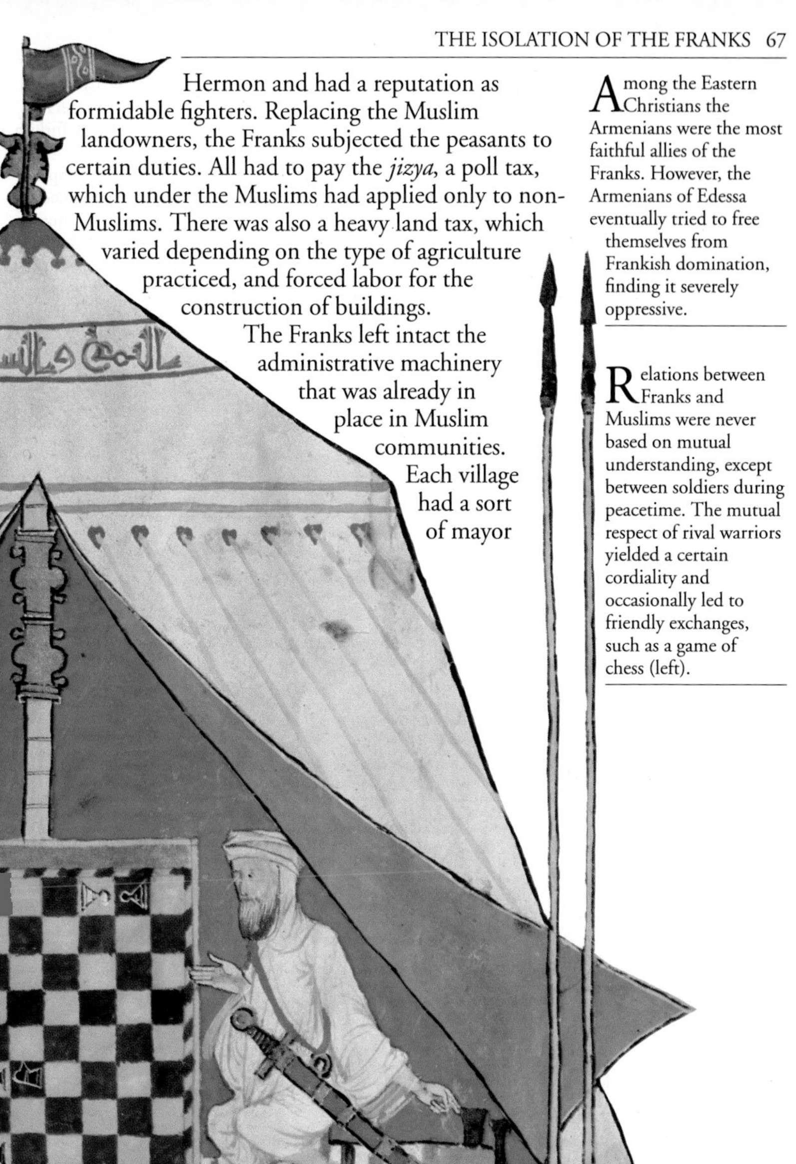

Among the Eastern Christians the Armenians were the most faithful allies of the Franks. However, the Armenians of Edessa eventually tried to free themselves from Frankish domination, finding it severely oppressive.

Relations between Franks and Muslims were never based on mutual understanding, except between soldiers during peacetime. The mutual respect of rival warriors yielded a certain cordiality and occasionally led to friendly exchanges, such as a game of chess (left).

Krak des Chevaliers (above and left), set on a height of the eastern slope of the Djebel Ansariya Mountains, made it possible to keep an eye on the Homs Pass, a strategic spot on the way to Egypt. When the crusaders captured it, it was an Arab castle. The count of Tripoli granted it to the Knights Hospitalers, who continually repaired it. The crusaders used the techniques and forms of Roman art in the churches that they built. Opposite: The cathedral of Tartus.

responsible for settling disputes and administering justice. He represented the village to the lord and collected taxes. At a higher level judicial affairs fell to the Franks.

Conciliatory Overtures to the Eastern Christians

The Franks attempted a sort of reconciliation with the Eastern Christians but their efforts failed because of

the elitism of the Franks. The Eastern Christians, organized into communities, obeyed their own clergy. The majority of these were Greek Orthodox and Jacobite Syrians. The Armenians had their own church but in 1198 officially recognized the authority of the pope.

The Franks showed a preference for the Syrian Christians over the Greek Orthodox, as the latter came from Constantinople and thus owed their allegiance to Byzantium —although they spoke Arabic. But on the whole the Franks displayed little flexibility; they formed a Latin ecclesiastical hierarchy and appropriated churches from the other Christian sects. Their treatment of the "non-Latins" became so intolerable that after three generations the Eastern Christians allied

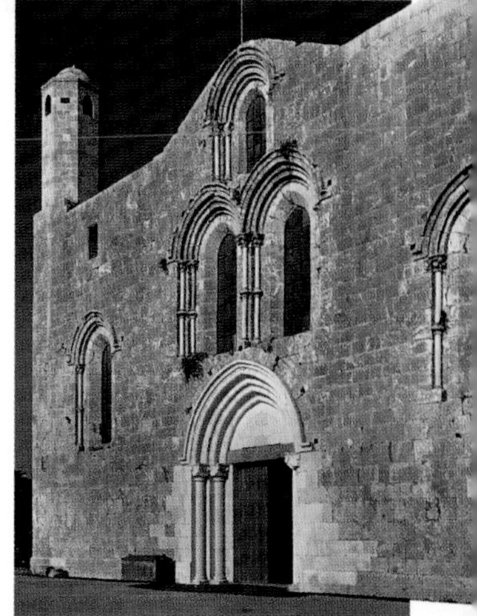

themselves with the Muslim leader Nureddin (Nur ad-Din), and then Saladin (Salah al-Din). Under the Muslims the Eastern Christians could at least expect a measure of autonomy. The Franks had now become their enemies, too.

Among the Eastern Christian communities, only the Maronites got along well with the crusaders. Living in the mountains overlooking Tripoli, the Maronites had provided the Franks with guides in 1099. They had disassociated themselves from the Christian Syrians in the 7th century. These mountain people were remarkable archers and good soldiers. They opened talks with the Frankish Church, and in 1182 Patriarch Aimery of Antioch effected the union of the Maronite and Roman churches.

Isolated in a foreign world, the Franks urgently needed to assert their unity. But more often they succeeded in doing exactly the opposite.

The Nobility Gradually Curtailed the Powers of the Latin Rulers

The first generation of nobles in the Latin settlements came from the ranks of the crusaders, but as they died out, their children and newcomers took over the government positions and fiefdoms. The richest among them formed an exclusive and powerful caste that reinforced itself through intermarriage. But the monarchy still authorized the consolidation of fiefdoms and expedited the concentration of landowners.

In 1131 Melisende, the first queen of Jerusalem, came to the throne after the death of her father

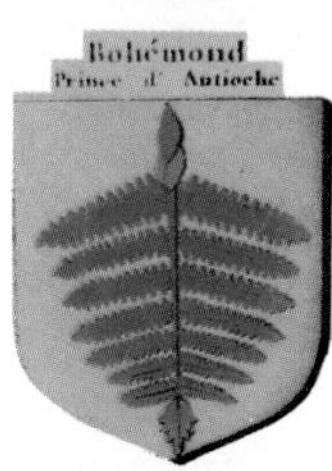

The coats of arms (left) of the great feudal lords—Godfrey of Bouillon, Bohemond, Raymond of Saint-Gilles, Hugh of Lusignan—proclaim their pride and power. The kings of Jerusalem preferred to rely on the nobles who had come from Europe rather than on the local aristocrats, whose power made them dangerous. Thus, Fulk of Anjou ascended to the throne through his marriage with Melisende (below), daughter of Baldwin II, and first queen of Jerusalem.

Baldwin II. She had married a wealthy French lord, Fulk of Anjou, who ruled with her as king. While Fulk oversaw a tremendous building program in the kingdom, including the completion of the church of the Holy Sepulcher, his reign was plagued by internal revolt.

Fulk clashed with a very powerful lord, Hugh of Le Puiset, who ruled the coastal fief of Jaffa, near Jerusalem. The reason for their argument is not clear, but some accounts claim that Hugh and the queen were having an affair. Fulk tried to get rid of Hugh by bringing him before the high court on trumped-up charges of treason. Hugh had the backing of many other nobles in his struggle against the king, but when he realized the seriousness of the charges against him, he foolishly called on Egyptian soldiers to help defend his fortified town. Appealing to the Muslims for help was indeed treasonous.

While Fulk favored the severest of punishments for Hugh's actions, the other nobles of the kingdom brought considerable pressure to bear on the king, and in the end Hugh was sentenced to a relatively lenient three-year exile. Fulk later quarreled with another nobleman, Roman of Le Puy, lord of Transjordan, and gave Le Puy's fief over to his butler. There are also indications that the queen and

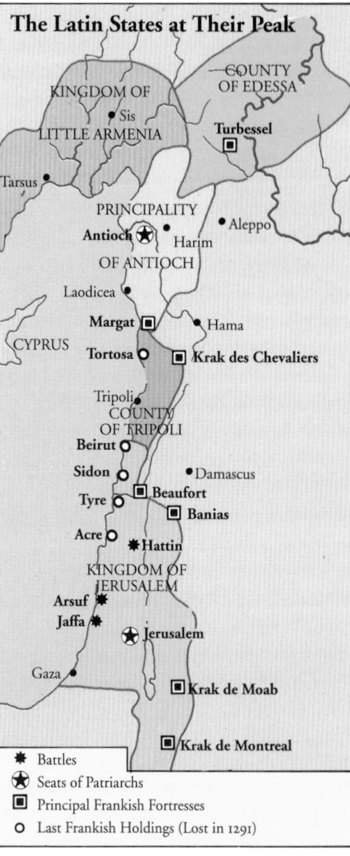

The Latin states covered a territory that was protected along one side by the coastal mountains: the Amanus, the Djebel Ansariya, and the Lebanon mountains. The ranges break off in the north, at the county of Edessa, in Upper Mesopotamia, and in the south on the Transjordanian plateau.

king, who were meant to rule jointly, were engaged in a power struggle themselves. These various conflicts served to undermine the power of the monarchy.

At the same time an increase in immigration meant that new fiefdoms had to be created. The original lords tried to obtain privileges denied to the new ones. A rivalry grew between great lords and simple knights, whose status had deteriorated since they were now awarded only estates instead of entire villages.

The knights fell under the protection of the great lords, whose power they increased. This enlarged the influence of a few lords, who managed to place limits on the king's power. Baldwin III could still confiscate fiefdoms under his own authority, but his successor, Amalric, could no longer do so. The power of the king of Jerusalem was definitely being challenged.

Sent to France and England by Baldwin II to seek help, Hugh of Payens, the founder of the Templars, was present at the Council of Troyes in 1128, when his new order, based on the Benedictines, was adopted. The Templars and the Hospitalers, which were also based on the Benedictine order, would later be criticized for their independence from both the king and the Church.

Templars and Hospitalers Leaned on the King

Hospices for pilgrims had been established along the routes leading from west to east even before the crusades. In the mid-11th century the merchants of Amalfi founded the Hospital of Saint John at Jerusalem, which gave its name to the Hospitalers. These institutions expanded after the capture of Jerusalem. Under Raymond of Le Puy, its second grand master, the Hospitalers became a military order. Since the Franks held only cities and fortresses, insecurity was rife throughout the kingdom, and the military orders, made up of lay brethren skilled in warfare,

provided needed protection.

Another chivalric order, the Templars, founded in 1119, was created to bring security to the area. Thus were combined two contrary vocations—military and monastic. The Templars were successful from the start. For their headquarters, the king gave them a section of Haram es-Sherif, "Solomon's Temple" of the crusaders. The order took its name from this temple. The Hospitalers and the Templars had the same status.

The orders played a decisive part in defending the area's borders, although this was not their initial purpose. They formed permanent armies whose ranks were constantly augmented by new recruits from the West. The defense of fortresses and castles—whose upkeep, much less enlargement, proved a financial burden too heavy for the monarchy or the lords—was handed over to the military orders. With the organization, quality, number, and permanent mobilization of their soldiers, the military orders should have been a formidable asset, but their growth proved politically disastrous for the Latin states, as they composed an independent and aggressive party whose goals did not always match those of the monarchy. They became too powerful to recede back into the ranks.

The shields of the Templars were embellished with a design in black and white (above). The knights adopted this insignia to remind them of their vows of poverty. However, the military order was actually very wealthy. Below: The tomb of a Knight Templar in an abbey in Dorchester, England. One of the first hospices for pilgrims is shown opposite above.

religion
le prince
de la passion
religion

“The order of the Templars comprised knights who would all become noble—sergeants from the middle class, squires or stewards, and clergy who served the chaplains. All took monastic vows; they were to have good weapons devoid of all ornament or gilding; over their hauberk [chain-mail tunic] floated a uniform, a coat that was white for knights, black for sergeants. Pope Eugenius III added a white cross, while the Hospitalers had a red cross. They wore their hair and beards short, to make it easier to see in front of and behind them. They were not allowed to fast for prolonged periods; on the contrary, they were expected to eat well in order to maintain their strength. The order was run by a veritable government, composed of a grand master and officers, but the important decisions could be made only by the Council of Knights.”

Louis Bréhier
L'Eglise et l'Orient au Moyen Age (*The Church and the East in the Middle Ages*), 1907

Left and opposite: Various ranks of the order of the Templars, including (opposite bottom left) a Dame Templar.

The ascendancy of the Muslim leader Zengi began a process of unification of Muslim Syria that would culminate under Nureddin. In 1144 Zengi conquered the county of Edessa and then all the non-Frankish states in Syria. Nureddin developed a coherent policy shaped by the ideology of the jihad—or holy war—and carried out by an organized military force.

CHAPTER IV

ZENGI, NUREDDIN, AND THE UNIFICATION OF SYRIA

The gardens and canals surrounding Damascus (opposite) made its access challenging for enemies. The Franks tried many times to take the city, but their persistent attacks only succeeded in driving Damascus into Nureddin's camp. Right: Two Muslim horsemen.

The Muslims and the Eastern Christians Were Both Now the Enemies of the Franks

The Franks had scandalized the East with their brutal and divisive behavior, but the civilian opposition to them had been disjointed. In 1104, after the Muslim victory at Harran, all the towns near Antioch populated by Eastern Christians opened their doors to the emir of Aleppo. In 1113 the Muslim population of Galilee revolted against their Frankish rulers and gave guides and provisions to the approaching Muslim army. In 1119, when Roger of Salerno, prince of Antioch, died at the "Field of Blood," the Christians of the city were on the verge of treason.

After about 1130, the Islamic world underwent a full-scale change in attitude.

Renaissance of the Ideology of the Jihad

Since the 7th century Syria had been considered the site of a holy war against Byzantium, but that campaign had lost its momentum. The ideology of a religious war resurfaced again after 1105 in Damascus and then in Aleppo, but it was still not a widespread movement.

But in 1124 things began to change. The Franks pressed Aleppo so hard that its emir abandoned the besieged city and appealed to Bursuq, emir of Mosul, for help and protection. Bursuq agreed on the condition that he be given Aleppo. Under pressure from the bourgeoisie and the common people, the emir of Aleppo agreed. Thus, plans for a promising union between Mosul and Aleppo were sketched out in 1125. Although Bursuq was killed by the Assassins, the union went forward in 1128 under Bursuq's successor, Zengi. This marked the beginning of a new period distinguished by the emirate of Zengi and the sultanate of Nureddin.

The Offensive Vigor of Zengi

While Zengi has been credited with advocating a holy war once he had Aleppo and Mosul, the jihad was neither the sole nor the principal goal of his policy. He was more concerned with insinuating his power into the heart of the Abbasid caliphate and the Persian sultanate. In fact his main goal at first was the capture of the

Damascus, Antioch, and Acre all served as Syrian capitals, in turn—and even simultaneously. Damascus, the historic capital, which has remained the capital of Muslim Syria, represented inland Syria. Antioch, capital of Roman and Byzantine Syria, was the seat of a Frankish principality. Acre played a short-lived but decisive role as capital of the second state of Jerusalem in the 13th century. It is shown on the map (opposite above), along with Jerusalem, with its Dome of the Rock. A camel suggests the proximity of the desert.

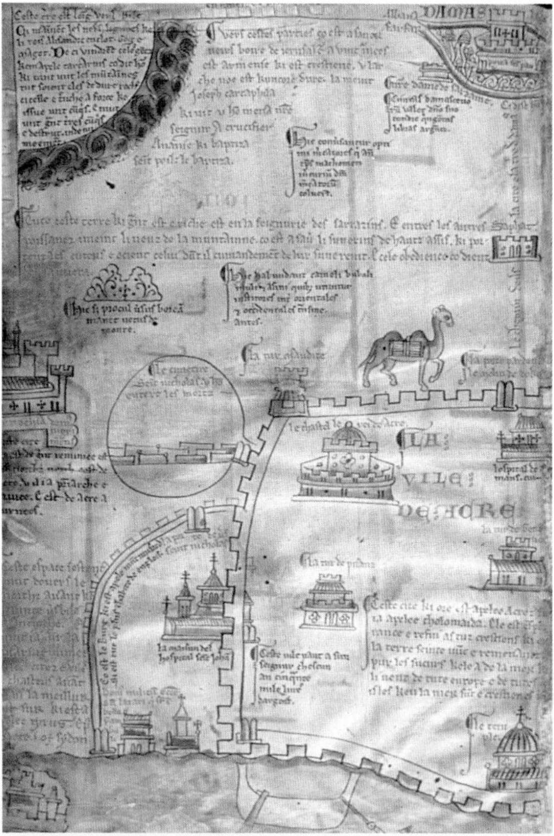

Below: Franks and Muslims face off. While this representation is set in a conventional western landscape, it is one of the few to emphasize the role of the infantry rather than the cavalry. It shows the importance of the archers on foot in both armies.

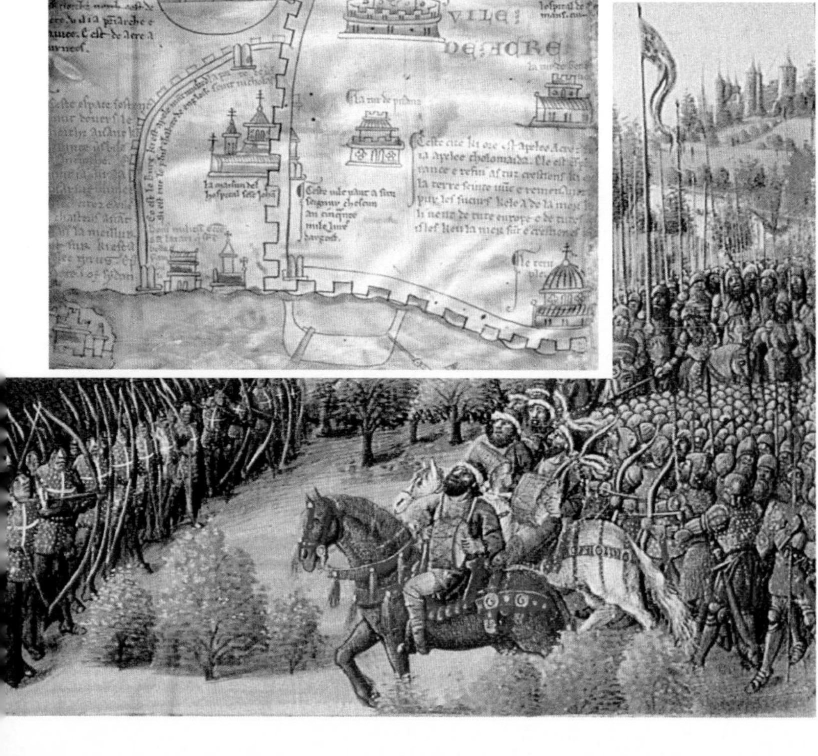

powerful state of Damascus. Zengi's primary distinction lay in the reunion of Aleppo and Mosul under his authority, on the one hand, and in the zeal and consistency with which he pursued his objectives, on the other. From the Franks he took a few small towns, thus gaining access to the plain of Antioch, but his major achievement was the conquest of all the Islamic towns and fortresses to the east of the Orontes River. In 1135 he failed to secure Damascus, which, although Muslim-ruled, maintained a tenuous but important tie to the king of Jerusalem. However, in only a few years he had halved the territory of the Latin states of the north.

Between 1135 and 1146 the Franks built fortresses in the south, encircling the town of Ashkelon, in Transjordan (the Krak of Moab), and in Galilee. In the same period Byzantine Emperor John II Comnenus and his army arrived in the north. After chasing the Turks from Anatolia, John II appeared before Antioch and forced the prince, Raymond of Poitiers, to acknowledge his sovereignty. Although all the crusading lords had sworn to give the lands they conquered to the Byzantine emperor, none of them kept his word. Raymond undertook to join John II in a campaign against Aleppo and Shaizar and agreed to take them in

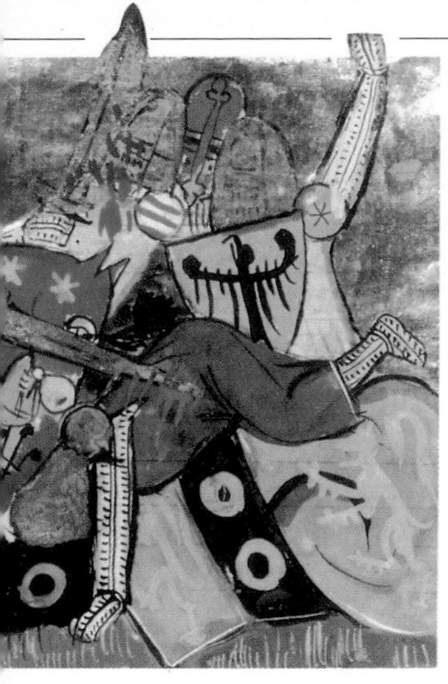

John's name only. The expedition did not succeed. Zengi pressed his advantage, taking Baalbek, but again failed to capture Damascus, which the Franks saved in 1139–40. The Damascenes and Franks recaptured Banias, which controlled communications between the emirate and the kingdom.

In 1142 John II returned to Syria, summoned by Raymond of Poitiers, but their alliance did not yield further results. John II wished to assert the empire's sovereignty over Antioch but, realizing that the Franks were now only agreeing to this because of the threat that Zengi represented, he gave them little help in repulsing the fierce emir.

Zengi came late to Syria. The son of a Turkish lieutenant to the great sultan Malik Shah, he distinguished himself first in Iraq in the service of the sultan of Persia, Mahmud, in the war against the caliph of Baghdad in 1127. As reward, he was named Iraq's high commissioner. Then he became governor of Mosul and was charged with taking up the struggle against the Franks. Throughout his career he retained the appearance of a brutal, unrefined Turkish captain, unlike his son, Nureddin, who had adopted the ways of a Syrian emir. For Zengi, the soldier always came before the politician. Left: The death of a western lord. Below: Muslim horsemen in formation.

The Fall of Edessa in 1144

Zengi thus found his way clear to Edessa; the Frankish control of this territory had presented a constant threat to communications between Aleppo and Mosul. The county had been greatly weakened after the Muslim slaughter of its inhabitants and the continual raids by its Muslim neighbors. Its army did not have a majority of Franks; while the many Armenians in its ranks offered sure loyalty and valor in the field, the same could scarcely be said of the Orthodox Syrians.

Taking advantage of the absence of Joscelin, count of Edessa, Zengi took the city in 1144, after a month-long siege. The first of the crusader states was now lost. He stopped his troops from massacring the remaining population and reassured the inhabitants of his good intentions by restoring their goods and returning to the Eastern Christians the churches taken over by the crusaders. He hoped to set a good example and thereby win the help of other Eastern Christians in his war against the West.

The failure of the Second Crusade was largely due to the behavior of Louis VII (opposite above), whose motives had more to do with appeasing his conscience than avenging the capture of Edessa and restabilizing the situation of the Latin states. On the crusade he acted like a pilgrim rather than a statesman. He was also jealous of the relationship between his wife, Eleanor of Aquitaine, and the prince of Antioch, Raymond of Poitiers. Instead of attacking Aleppo, where Raymond had asked for his support, he hurried to Jerusalem to present himself as a pilgrim.

But Zengi was murdered by a fellow Muslim on 15 September 1146. That same year the Armenians of Edessa with links to the Franks revolted. After resecuring the city, the Muslims killed or drove away the Armenians and replaced them with Jews, in whom Nureddin, Zengi's son and successor, had more confidence.

The Defeat of the Second Crusade

The fall of Edessa elicited a call for a new crusade from the West. Unlike the first, it was not the pope but the Cistercian Abbot Bernard of Clairvaux, a leading Church intellectual, who made the appeal, and it was organized by sovereigns Louis VII, king of France, and Conrad III, German emperor.

Saint Bernard, a most eloquent speaker and "sweet-tongued teacher," was so persuasive that during one of his speeches he ran out of the cloth crosses he had brought to hand out to the crowds and had to tear his habit up into strips. About twenty-five thousand crusaders left; of which no more than five thousand arrived in Syria in the spring of 1148. The German army was virtually exterminated while crossing Asia Minor, and the French suffered constant harassment all the way down the coast. Raymond of Poitiers advised Louis VII to head directly for Aleppo in order to meet Nureddin in full force and recapture the places they had lost beyond

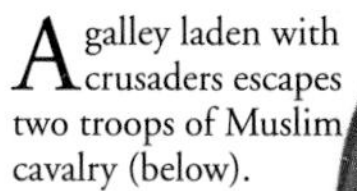

A galley laden with crusaders escapes two troops of Muslim cavalry (below).

the Orontes. Instead of following this wise advice Louis went straight to Jerusalem and was persuaded to march on to Damascus, which he could not take. Conrad III and his men set sail for home in September 1148; six months later, Louis followed. The Second Crusade failed, eroding the myth of the Franks' invincibility.

Nureddin United the Muslim Lords of Syria

From 1151 to 1157 Nureddin realized his father's goal. He secured all the towns and fortresses beyond the Orontes River, notably Homs. On 29 June 1149 he defeated Raymond of Poitiers, prince of Antioch, and took most of the territory belonging to Antioch, leaving the capital on the border. This was his finest victory against the West and greatly boosted Nureddin's standing in the Muslim world. What remained of the county of Edessa

fell to his control, and in 1154 he took Damascus. For the first time in centuries Muslim Syria experienced political unity. Its borders had been extended to Mosul, Harran, and, to the north, as far as the Taurus Mountains.

Between 1157 and 1160 Nureddin's advance slowed down a pace. The prince of Antioch recaptured Harim, creating more space for his territory.

Baldwin III, king of Jerusalem, had turned to Byzantium for help. The large Greek Orthodox population of northern Syria made the future of the region of some concern to the Byzantines, and Baldwin III, determined to guarantee their involvement,

In spring 1149 Nureddin attacked the principality of Antioch with six thousand cavalry. Raymond of Poitiers, prince of Antioch, intended to hold him at bay with a force of four hundred cavalry and one thousand foot soldiers. He managed to surprise Nureddin and carried off the first victory. Instead of waiting for reinforcements within the safety of a castle, however, he camped in open country. A Shia chief who had left Nureddin's camp to join the Franks tried in vain to dissuade Raymond from continuing without reinforcements. Meanwhile, Nureddin had learned from his spies of the enemy's weakness. In the morning, the Franks found themselves surrounded, with no chance of escape, and were crushed (left). The 12th-century Arab historian Ibn al-Qalansi reported: "The body of the unlucky prince was found stretched out amid the corpses of his most valorous knights. His head was cut off and brought to Nureddin. He was one of the most celebrated of the Franks for his great bravery, extraordinary strength, and unusual height. He was no less famous for his arrogance and brutality."

Opposite: The capture of Ashkelon in 1153.

requested the hand in marriage of a niece of Byzantine Emperor Manuel I. Baldwin's brother and successor, Amalric, made a similar alliance and Manuel himself married Maria of Antioch. Further, the king of Jerusalem forced Reginald of Châtillon, prince of Antioch, to officially recognize Byzantium's sovereignty. Manuel entered the city and took over the fortress. However, these elaborate alliances proved as superficial as all those before them; a joint expedition against Nureddin petered out twenty-five miles from Antioch. Like John II, Manuel found it more expedient to contain rather than destroy the Muslim threat. The subtle diplomacy of the Byzantine emperor

succeeded in bringing about a delicate balance of power between all sides, which was maintained for a few years. The Franks actually held back major attacks for a time while Nureddin dealt with another problem, shared by them all—the Seljuk Turks in Anatolia.

By 1160 Nureddin was back on the offensive. He captured Reginald of Châtillon and Joscelin III of Edessa and then took back all the lands that he had just lost. All the while he maintained a constant pressure on the Latin states through guerrilla operations and extended his domain beyond Syria—to Mosul in 1170, then Upper Mesopotamia, Anatolia, and even Cilicia, where he interrupted struggles over the succession of Thoros II among Armenian princes, Byzantines, and Franks and seized sites from the Templars.

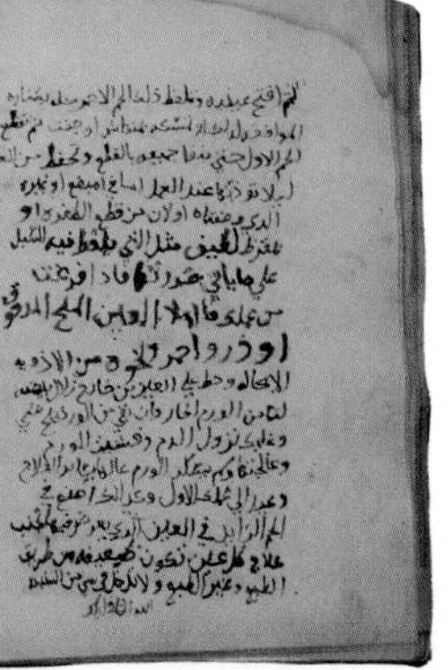

The Grandeur of Nureddin's Principality

For the first time since the Franks won Jerusalem, Muslim Syria found itself under a single ruler, Nureddin. He could not have accomplished this goal without using force, but it would not have worked without a radical change in public opinion. The populations of the cities under Islamic rule—Christian, Jewish, and Muslim—found themselves worn out by the doings of the Franks. Not only did the latter refuse to assimilate, thus emaining foreigners in their lands, they also carried on a constant war against the inland areas of Syria, creating a state of perpetual insecurity. Although they had not stopped the trade caravans crossing their territory, they taxed them heavily. Traders between the East and the Mediterranean had to develop new routes to avoid the Latin states.

Nureddin was Turkish and, like the Franks, was considered a foreigner by the Arab populations of Syria. Unlike the Franks, however, he was shrewd enough to respect the organization and workings of the local societies; he controlled them while drawing support from the principles that governed them. Above all else, he was Muslim. As long as he observed the laws of Islam and respected its traditions, there was no obstacle to a foreigner

Arab medicine was far more advanced than European medicine until the end of the Middle Ages (left, several extracts from a 7th-century treatise on pathology). Learned Muslims had inherited ancient texts, especially Greek ones, and the empirical expertise of their pharmacists arose from a purely eastern tradition (Mesopotamian and Egyptian), transmitted orally. On the battlefield, however, the wounded barely benefited from this superior knowledge, unless they were wealthy or from the upper ranks. In the Islamic army, as in the Frankish army, more soldiers died from lack of care than from the severity of their wounds.

Nureddin (shown bathing opposite), second son of Zengi, inherited many of his father's characteristics: rigor, courage, and a strong sense of state. He succeeded in bringing his virtues to bear on his political activity in the service of the jihad.

ruling over the region. In this way the Turks gradually integrated themselves into Arab society. The Turks could rule them and unify them since they did not overturn the existing order.

In the Islamic world gatherings played an important social role and were often conducted in public places.

Nureddin Developed a Coherent Policy Founded on the Jihad

At first the Muslims had considered their struggles with the crusaders, and before them the Byzantines, as wars of expansion—they were not strictly speaking "holy wars." This changed under Nureddin; the war against the Christians had now become a religious war. Nureddin, who was also a religious zealot, viewed the jihad as both ideology and policy. The ideology emphasized three basic points: the depth of the gulf separating Franks and Muslims; a protest against the indifference of their contemporaries to that fact; and a call to holy war. Zengi had begun to articulate these ideas; just before taking

Edessa, he stressed the absolute necessity of leading an offensive war against the Franks, without equivocation and to the death, until they were completely gone. Nureddin elaborated the idea of the jihad into a complete theory, sketching out a precise political path, and put in place an extensive apparatus to ensure its spread. He emphasized the special sanctity of Jerusalem and the Holy Land and the need to re-establish the political unity of the Islamic Near East as the preliminary phase to driving out the Franks. The jihad thus rested on a strong spiritual movement that had been fermenting for a century—the re-establishment of Sunnism. This became the basis of an important popular movement.

In the 13th century Aleppo contained 208 *masjids*, small neighborhood mosques, plus 10 on the outer wall and 300 in the surrounding towns. After the mosque, the most common religious monument was the *madrasa*.

Above: Miniature painting of a man seated in his house.

A Propaganda Machine

In Islam's earliest days, all teaching, religious and nonreligious, took place in the mosque, in accordance with Sunni theory. Starting in the 11th century, when the Sunni countermovement was on the rise, the Seljuks developed religious schools, called *madrasas*, as institutions of the state. Nureddin increased their numbers. When he took power, there were sixteen; he created forty-two more, and he appointed their teachers as well. The main subject taught in the *madrasas* was the law, or *fiqh*. These schools functioned as active seats for the spread of Sunnism and the ideology of the jihad.

The *hadiths*, records of the behavior and words of the Prophet Muhammad, were introduced into Syria by Nureddin. They performed the same instructive role as the *madrasas* and became widespread. Sufism, a mystical Islamic philosophy, flourished during the Sunni revival.

In addition to these institutions, Nureddin relied on propagandists, voluntary or professional, to sing his praises, broadcasting the goals of his policies while exalting his person. An entire literary production—poetry, letters, treatises—developed in his honor. Nureddin was celebrated as "fire for the infidels and light for the religion." One of his eulogists exclaimed, "While all the other sovereigns think of nothing but defending their empty worldly goods, you dedicate yourself to the defense of religion." This propaganda made its way into inscriptions found on various buildings, such as "Guardian of Allah's land" and "Conqueror of infidels and pagans."

Islamic culture, like the Byzantine, was based on writing (left, a 12th-century Syrian inkwell). When the crusaders took Constantinople in 1204, some of them went around the city pretending to write. They were mocking the Byzantines because nothing seemed more ridiculous to them than writing. Between the East and the West lay a vast cultural chasm, which widened in the course of the 13th century and grew more pronounced in the 14th and 15th centuries. Below: Two men drinking. Opposite: A man hunting.

An Effective Government Thanks to Swift and Frequent Communications

In order to be effective, Nureddin's method of governing required efficient means of communication. He imposed on the emirates under his control an administrative and fiscal apparatus whose furthest reaches were linked by an elaborate courier system. The courier was responsible

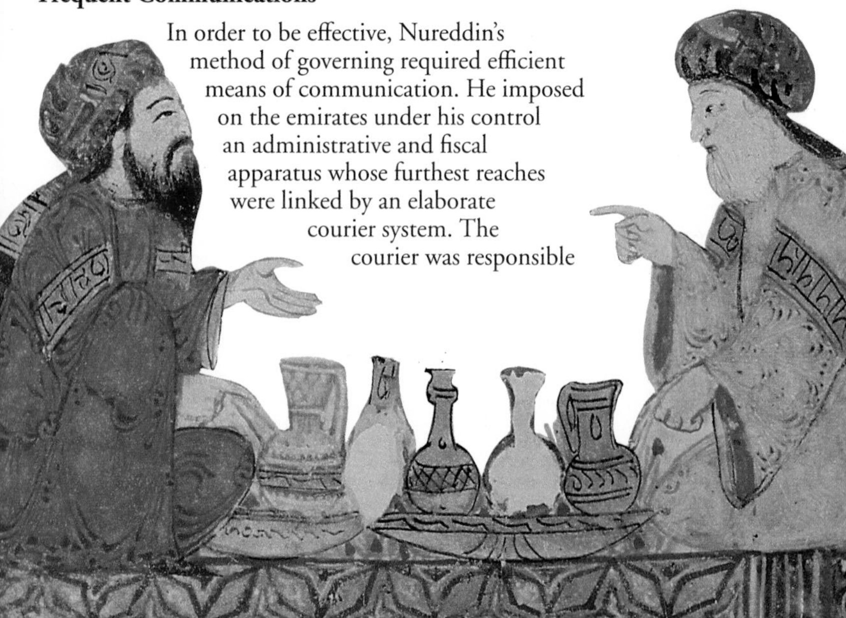

for writing out, recording, and circulating dispatches among the governors. This system dated back to ancient times, but it had lost its effectiveness with the decline of the Abbasid caliphate. Nureddin updated it, using horses and, for certain routes, camels. His great innovation, however, was creating a carrier-pigeon communication system, which guaranteed him a decisive edge over the Franks by assuring the quick transmission of orders and information.

The administration of civil law remained light-handed. It was headed by a vizier, who enjoyed considerably less power than his counterpart in the Abbasid period. Starting out as a sort of secretary of state, he was gradually reduced to the level of treasurer, responsible for keeping an eye on the tax collectors and consolidating all the taxes. He retained the status of a political advisor and received as payment about ten percent of the state's revenues. Another important figure, the chamberlain, evolved from a ceremonial figurehead to a real head of government. He also regulated the police and the flow of information, acting as a sort of minister of the interior.

Each Citadel in the Empire Served as the Seat of a Governor

Nureddin selected the governor, a soldier chosen from among the most faithful emirs, to act as the true ruler of a city and region. His salary sometimes took the form of a fee and a fixed amount of agricultural products delivered regularly. The governors were carefully watched by spies to forestall uprisings.

In major cities judges or *naibs* exercised military

"My father—God have pity on him!—chased roe deer on the lands near the fortress. As he was chasing the last deer, his mare's hoof got caught in one of those pits dug to catch wild boar. While falling on my father, she broke his collarbone. She righted herself, galloped twenty cubits—my father remaining stretched out—then returned, stopped right beside him, cried and neighed until he picked himself up and his servants ran to put him back in the saddle. This is how Arab horses behave."

Ouzama, *Hunting Stories*

authority and, as such, supervised the collection of taxes and maintained order.

These high-ranking officials were given big responsibilities. Their nomination gave rise to a solemn ceremony that included the presentation of a robe of honor, made from cloth woven in state workshops, as in Byzantium, whose colors reflected the importance of their position. In addition they received a chain and other gifts, including a horse and a richly embellished sword, and a diploma of investiture. The impressive ritual, arranged by Nureddin, expressed the *naib*'s supreme dignity, the legitimacy of his powers, and the greatness of his rank.

His Resources Made Nureddin One of the Greatest Princes of His Day

The government operated under a sound fiscal policy. The system had changed little from ancient times; three canonical taxes remained in full effect. The *jizya* affected only non-Muslims. While relatively light, this tax fell mostly on the poor. The *zakat*, an obligatory alms, was among the main obligations of Islam. The principal tax was the *kharaj*, tied to property and agricultural production. To these standard taxes were added occasional taxes, including a portion of booty (generally one-fifth), and those taxes and duties not administered by Muslim law, most of which involved commercial transactions.

The management of the state's resources was carried out by a large and competent administration, although it did not always gather taxes directly. In many cases it called on farmers, who advanced the total amount of taxes minus a certain percentage that they earned, for collecting the rest.

This fiscal system allowed Nureddin to fulfill all his obligations as a Muslim, leaving him with significant sums to finance a

The weakening of the caliph's power and the development of local dynasties encouraged the growth of a Muslim middle class. In each town where a dynasty held sway, the middle class prospered by filling the needs of the new leaders. Above: A Syrian goblet from the mid-12th century. Left: Syrian and Egyptian coins.

sumptuous court worthy of his rank and maintain a strong army and an active propaganda service—all without delving into his secret funds.

His policies had the desired effect: In Aleppo, the Shias dropped into the minority, and in Damascus the Assassins lost support. Nureddin had understood the power of a united Syria.

"He who lets himself be dominated by others and suffers humiliations will come to rue it. He who does not take up arms to defend his cistern will see it destroyed. He who does not attack will be attacked."

In 1164 Egypt Became the Principal Prize of War

The key to King Amalric's policy centered on the control of Egypt. The Franks no longer thought about establishing a Christian government in Egypt, but they needed at least an ally or a protectorate there. Since the beginning of the century, Egypt had steadily grown weaker. If Nureddin could secure it, his power would become irresistible and Jerusalem would be surrounded by Islam. The initiative came from the Egyptians themselves. In 1164 Shawar, a vizier of upper Egypt who had taken refuge in Syria, convinced Nureddin to overthrow the Shia Fatimids and reestablish a Sunni government. Nureddin entrusted this mission to his Kurdish lieutenant, Shirkuh, who accomplished it easily at the head of a troop of Turkomans. But once he reassumed his role as vizier, Shawar fell out with Shirkuh and sent an appeal to the Franks. Amalric of Jerusalem besieged Shirkuh at Bilbeis and would have taken the city if he had not been called back to Jerusalem to respond to Nureddin's capture of Harim in the principality of Antioch. Shirkuh tried again in 1167 to push out Shawar, but he fared no better, as Amalric advanced as far as Cairo. Again Nureddin staged a diversionary

attack, this time on the county of Tripoli, and both armies retired from the field. But Amalric won a large tribute in gold pieces from Egypt, and he left a Frankish governor in Cairo and garrisons to oversee the collection of the tribute.

This quick success inspired the Franks to venture further. In 1168 Amalric prepared an expedition to take over Egypt without an invitation from any of the Egyptian factions. The military orders played a decisive role in this decision, marking the entry of a new pressure group, a true war party. Before going ahead with his attack, Amalric made diplomatic overtures to Byzantium. They agreed to conquer Egypt together and share the spoils as well as, perhaps, the country. In 1168 Amalric put the understanding into an official document.

Meanwhile Shawar made a new alliance with Nureddin and Shirkuh. The Franks took Bilbeis and then besieged Cairo, but Shirkuh and Saladin, his nephew, arrived unexpectedly in January 1169, and the Franks were forced to retreat. Worse than the loss of Egypt was the formation of an immense state, stretching from the Euphrates to the Nile, opposite

“Already Baldwin II had benefited from the civil wars in Cairo by wringing from the Fatimid government the promise of 160,000 deniers in tribute. Amalric used the nonpayment of this tribute as a pretext to invade the Delta in September 1163. He crossed the isthmus of Suez without any trouble, challenged the army of Dirgham on the banks of the Pelusiac Branch, and lay siege to Bilbeis (opposite). A part of the ramparts had already fallen to him when Dirgham, taking advantage of the swelling of the Nile, smashed the dikes and caused a flood that forced the Franks to retreat.”

the Latin states. After the death of Shirkuh, Saladin had Shawar assassinated, appropriated the title of vizier, and, with the help of his Turkish force, took over the government.

Saladin, Lieutenant of Nureddin, in Egypt

Once in power, although in the name of Nureddin, Saladin abolished the Fatimid caliphate, founded Sunni *madrasas*, and announced Egypt's return to the Abbasid caliphate. The Egyptians, who did not have a deep attachment to Shiism, rallied around the new regime. Saladin took the title of *malik* (king), annexed upper Egypt, and sent an expedition to Yemen. He forcefully asserted his domination of Egypt, which made him a rival to Nureddin. The latter tried, without success, to bring him to heel. He summoned Saladin to join him in an attack on the Turkish fortresses of Transjordan. While Saladin complied, in 1171 and 1173, each time he withdrew after a brief display of force. Nureddin decided to invade Egypt to remove his lieutenant, but he fell ill and died on 15 May 1174, leaving Saladin the main force of Islam.

"From that moment, Amalric conceived the project to conquer Egypt and, in a letter, revealed his plan to the king of France, Louis VII (opposite). 'As we cherish your person and your kingdom and are devoted to your service and have invested special hopes in you and your kingdom, we deem it fitting to inform you of the success of our arms.... If, therefore, your magnificent virtue is inclined to give us aid, Egypt could easily be marked with the sign of the Cross.'"

René Grousset
L'Epopée des croisades
(The Epic of the Crusades),
1939

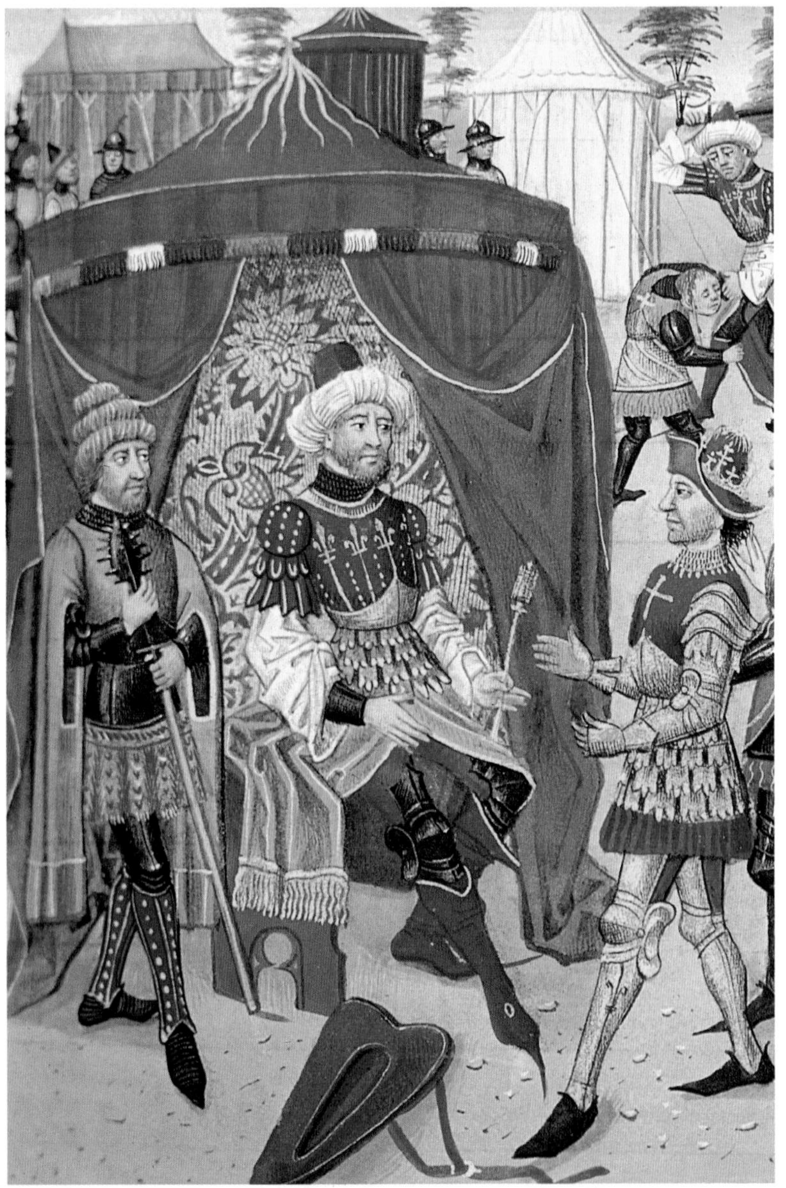

Saladin took over Nureddin's program in full (including marrying his widow), but on an even larger scale. He came very close to succeeding: He crushed the Franks at Hattin and took back Jerusalem. A third crusade gave the Franks the means to hang onto the coast, where they remained for another century. Despite further attempts to regain their grounds, their fate was sealed. They were driven out in 1291.

CHAPTER V

SALADIN'S VICTORY

Saladin was the strongest personality of his time. His courage and loyalty evoked both admiration and jealousy in enemy and ally alike. He is pictured, opposite, setting free the king of Jerusalem after the battle of Hattin, and at right, wielding a sword.

Saladin Made No Headway Against the Zengids Until 1180

When Nureddin died, Saladin controlled only Egypt. Starting in 1174, he took over Damascus, Homs, Hama, then three-quarters of Syria. His attempt to unify Egypt and Syria came up against the resistance of Aleppo. It took him nine years, from 1174 to 1183, to form the largest empire of the Near East since the Seljuks, meeting numerous adversaries: the Franks, with whom he fought every year; the Zengids—the followers of Zengi and his son Nureddin—who held Aleppo and Mosul and considered him a usurper; and, a subsidiary but real threat, the Assassins, a Shia Muslim sect that sought to murder him.

The first initiative against him came from the Franks. Although Baldwin IV of Jerusalem, who had succeeded Amalric, was ill with leprosy, the strength and energy of the Frankish army kept Saladin in check for a long time. They did everything they could to prevent the defeat of the Zengids, realizing such an outcome would make Saladin an invincible opponent. Their diversionary tactics worked: In 1176 Saladin gave up his attacks on Aleppo. The Franks even envisioned striking him in Egypt.

Further north, at Myriocephalum in 1176, a huge Seljuk army defeated the Byzantine Emperor Manuel I Comnenus, whose protectorate of the northern principalities posed a permanent threat to Islam. The defeat was colossal and the Byzantine position completely undermined. Desperate to win back some ground Manuel offered his fleet to the Franks for a joint venture against Egypt, but their disagreements kept the project from being realized. From here on the Franks would have to survive without Byzantium.

The initiative passed to Saladin, who kept up his attacks against the Franks, victories following defeats. The Franks held onto their major positions but suffered serious losses in the heart of their territories. The Egyptian fleet even made its way to Acre, now the most important port of the Latin East. Attacked on all sides, the Franks

Small, delicate, his beard short and even, his expression thoughtful, courteous, and chivalrous: This is how his contemporaries depicted Saladin (below), who strove to prove himself a worthy successor to Nureddin.

After deposing the Fatimids in Egypt (left), Saladin attempted the invasion of Syria in the name of Islamic unity, which was essential if the jihad against the Franks was to succeed. Saladin's sincerity was questioned in his time by the Zengids and the Abbasids and more recently by some historians. Joshua Prawer believes it was the Franks' insistence on fighting, in disastrous conditions, the heaviest concentration of Islamic troops ever brought together that enabled Saladin to destroy the kingdom of Jerusalem.

obtained a truce in 1180. Saladin's success against the Franks reinforced his prestige in the Muslim world. He accused the Zengids of treason, but they stood their ground with the support of Aleppo and Mosul.

In 1181 the Franks Took Up the Banner Again, but Saladin Came Out Ahead and Conquered Aleppo in 1183

The Frankish monarchy grew weaker. Freed after sixteen years of captivity at Aleppo, Reginald of Châtillon became lord of Transjordan. From the two mighty fortresses there at Montreal and Moab, he controlled the road from Damascus to Mecca, which passed through Egypt and was crucial to Saladin. A plundering

knight with an aggressive, daredevil temperament, Reginald was given to bold and rash actions. In 1181 he violated the truce by marching on the oasis of Taima, not far from the Muslim holy city of Medina, hoping to attack. A diversionary attack forced him back on the road. When he returned the next day, he plundered a very rich caravan and made away with a booty of 200,000 gold pieces. In defiance of Baldwin IV's orders, he refused to return it to Saladin. The war was on.

Saladin attacked and lay waste Samaria, while the royal army was in Transjordan. He accused the Zengids of colluding with the Franks as the latter, taking advantage of the situation, took Hama and threatened Damascus. Saladin's response was a crushing blow: In June 1183 he took Aleppo, the last link in Syrian-Egyptian unity. His holdings now stretched to Yemen and the eastern borders of Tunisia.

Saladin's reputation was exalted even among his Christian enemies. His generosity toward the Frankish populations and his chivalrous gestures overrode the cold-blooded massacres he ordered after the battle of Harim in 1178, after the coastal attacks of Reginald of Châtillon in 1183, and in fighting subsequent to the battle of Hattin. At left, he is shown looking on as the eyes of a Frank are torn out.

Saladin Forced the Franks to Request a New Truce

For the Franks the war took on an inexorable nature. In winter 1182 Reginald of Châtillon made the first offensive move in a grandiose and crazy project. He transported ships by camel to Aelana (present-day Eilat, Israel), a port on the Red Sea, which he took over, then went along the Arab coast and pillaged Egyptian and Arab ports, and finally marched on Medina. The Muslims found this an intolerable outrage. Saladin took advantage of the situation by becoming the avenger of Islam: He captured and killed every member of the expedition except for Reginald of Châtillon, who managed to escape. In September 1183 Saladin destroyed Galilee and seized several castles. Led by Guy of Lusignan, brother-in-law of and designated successor to Baldwin IV, the Franks stuck to a defensive strategy that forced Saladin to retreat.

The Muslim leader submitted them to a new type of warfare: When the Franks were weakened by a scarcity of provisions, he attacked them simultaneously on land and at sea. In 1185 Saladin granted them a four-year truce. On the face of it he had failed to secure his objectives. While he had reunited Egypt and Syria under his

The sect of the Assassins twice attempted to kill Saladin, who initially responded by attacking them, unsuccessfully, in their hideout. He next sought a reconciliation, thus depriving his enemies, Frankish and Muslim, of their support. Below: Saladin's cavalry.

control, he proved unable to destroy the western army or even win a single fortified location in Transjordan. During this time the Franks, it seemed, had demonstrated the effectiveness of their defense. The reality, however, was considerably different.

In 1185 Saladin's Forces Grew Mighty

Saladin welcomed the break in the fighting because he wanted to capture Mosul and he needed time. He already controlled a vast empire and had at his command more than eight thousand Egyptian cavalry, to which he added the border Arabs and six thousand Syrian cavalry. The Egyptian army contained well-trained and seasoned Kurdish and Turkish warriors, and the Syrian army had proved itself in battle.

Against this army the Franks had no more than one thousand knights. Their armor gave them an advantage even with fewer men, but Saladin had so many men at his disposal that he could afford to replace those lost, while a single Frankish defeat could prove irreparable.

Saladin had also rebuilt the Egyptian fleet so that it could block Palestinian ports and permanently impair the Franks' ability to replenish supplies. He had almost the same war equipment as the Franks, with one exception: "Greek fire," a mixture containing naphtha that could burn on water. The Franks had not yet discovered this weapon—an early form of napalm—which wreaked havoc in siege situations. However, Saladin lacked wood for building ships, and his soldiers'

As soon as the campaign ended and the possibilities of pillaging had been exhausted, the contingents that made up Saladin's army returned to their emirates. This practice, along with a lack of funds, made it difficult for Saladin to capitalize on his successes. The jealousy that his victories aroused in the Muslim world may be another reason for this situation. Below: An Arab horseman.

swords were not as strong as the ones used by the Franks. In order to obtain better swords he cultivated relations with the Italian republics; he was amused at the prospect of getting arms from the Franks to use against other Franks.

Saladin's one weak point was in the deployment of his resources. He did not have a standing army—which would have been a huge expense—but instead a conglomerate made up of soldiers who were assembled for each campaign. Once their objective was achieved, the soldiers dispersed and returned to their local emirs.

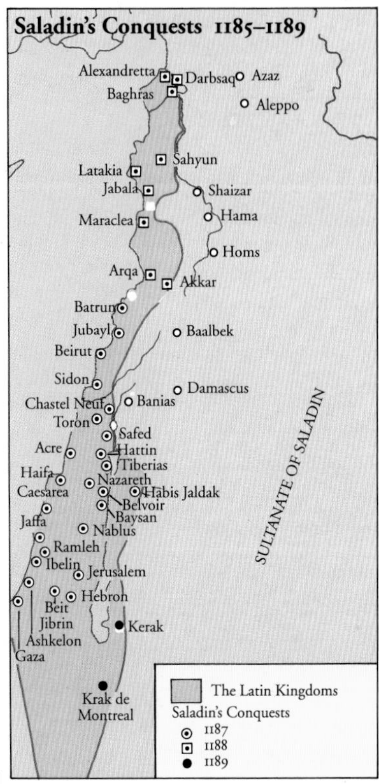

Through the offer of generous terms of surrender as well as the use of force, Saladin captured all the Frankish towns and fortresses except Tripoli, Antioch, and Tyre, successfully defended by Conrad of Montferrat. The sultan made a triumphant entry into Jerusalem on 2 October 1187.

While Saladin's Strength Grew, That of the Franks Declined

The war drained the Franks. It pinpointed their vulnerability to attacks on several fronts. In 1183 the high court of Jerusalem decided to impose a tax on both property and revenues throughout the kingdom. In 1184 the patriarch of Jerusalem, as well as the grand masters of the Templars and the Hospitalers, traveled west—to Constantinople, as well as to France and England—to sound the alarm. But their appeal went unheeded and no help was forthcoming. The Franks found themselves alone against Saladin. A successful resistance depended on a totally unified government, which was far from the case. The kingdom of Jerusalem was divided into two competing "parties" both vying for the king's power and influence. At the forefront were the old Syrian-Palestine nobility, who were mocked by the newcomers for their adoption of certain eastern customs. These long-

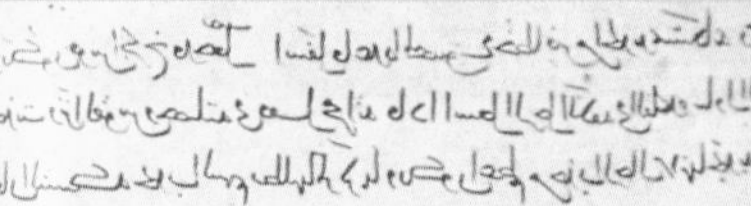

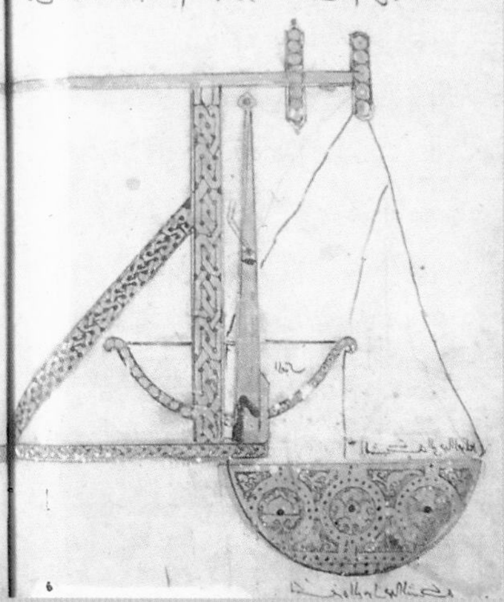

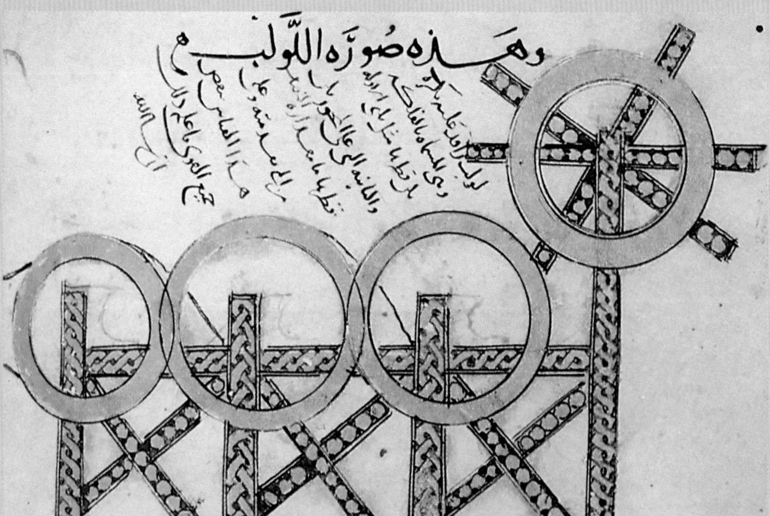

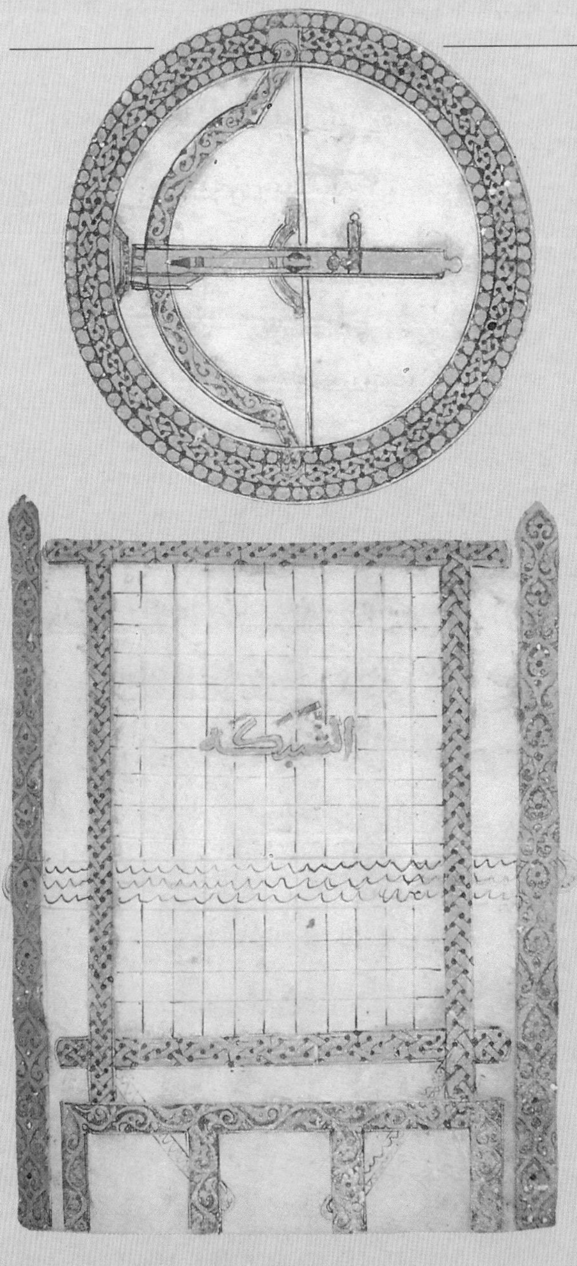

War, an Art and a Science

The dynasties of the Ayyubids and Mamluks generated many treatises on the ways to wage war. At the end of the 12th century Mardi Ibn al-Tartusi edited a short and very specific manual for Saladin that examined the different weapons, the techniques of fighting, and the ways of setting siege. Some of the inventions seem superfluous, such as the combination shield/ crossbow (above left). A more useful invention was the mobile shelter, which offered protection to soldiers by means of a grid of ropes stretched across a wooden frame-shield (left). A Persian mangonel—for catapulting stones and other projectiles—which works by counterweights, is pictured opposite above. Opposite below: The crossbow tower.

ألقاها على الغريم سرعة وإلا تحرقه ويكون زجاجها بقوة
حتى تنكسر على الخصم فإنها أي موضع وقعت عليه أحرقته ولا يطفى نارها
إلا بالخل

وصفه وهذه صفتها

وهذه القوارير تعليم الخضر للاسكندر

Crossbows and Greek Fire

Launched at the enemy in clay pots, "Greek fire" (opposite above) was used in naval combat (above) and during sieges to set fire to war machines (below, a catapult). Composed of sulfur, saltpeter, and oil of naphtha, "Greek fire" can burn on water. Its invention has been attributed to a Syrian of the 9th century, Callinicus, who imparted his secret to the Byzantine emperor. The Muslims used it to great effect against the crusaders. The westerners did not learn the secret of its composition until much later. Invented at the end of the Roman era, the crossbow (opposite below) was perfected in Italy during the Middle Ages. Although slower than a longbow, it could be shot more accurately and had a powerful force at long range. It was so murderously effective that its use was outlawed by the second Lateran Council in 1139 except for use against the infidels.

Since Baldwin IV could not have any children, his succession was to revert to the husband of one of his sisters—Sibylla, who was a widow, or, by default, Isabella. Isabella had married Humphrey of Toron, a member of the old nobility who had none of the qualities necessary to a king. The court became a nest of intrigue, and the physical weakness of the king left the field open to Reginald of Châtillon and a newcomer, Guy of Lusignan, who seduced Sibylla. In 1180, in precarious health, Baldwin IV consented to his sister's marriage to Guy of Lusignan (left), despite the latter's inexperience and lack of stature. In 1183 he named him regent but, disappointed by his ineptness and arrogance, soon removed him and named Guy's enemy, Raymond of Tripoli, reputed to be the most knowledgeable man in the kingdom. As his successor, Baldwin designated the son from Sibylla's first marriage. On Baldwin IV's death, Baldwin V was crowned king, at the age of five or six years (opposite above).

established lords, led by Raymond III, count of Tripoli, had managed to turn their domains into semi-autonomous states. The high court had become the exclusive organ of the high nobility, for the lesser nobles could no longer set forth their own opinions. (This "party" was itself divided into rival factions corresponding to the great families.)

Opposite this powerful group was the "court party." Its members were nobles recently arrived from the West. The military orders, the Templars and Hospitalers, although rivals themselves, became part of this party. They represented a military and political force of substantial influence, and while they supported the king, they pushed him toward risky undertakings.

A New King of Jerusalem

The question of the succession to Baldwin IV, the "Leper King," began during his lifetime. The legitimate heir was Baldwin V,

After only a few months of nominal rule, Baldwin V also died. The regency remained with Raymond III of Tripoli, who had the support of the Frankish lords of Syria. But Guy of Lusignan had on his side the patriarch of Jerusalem, Gerard of Ridefort—grand master of the Templars—Reginald of Châtillon, and Joscelin of Courtenay. In 1186 he succeeded in having himself crowned king of Jerusalem by the patriarch. In the interest of keeping the split from widening, Raymond III refrained from intervening. However, he made overtures to Saladin, which weakened his ethical stance. After Saladin's attack on Galilee in 1187, Guy and Raymond were reconciled (below).

son of the king's sister Sibylla, widow of William of Montferrat. Sibylla, however, fell in love with a young knight from the West, Guy of Lusignan, and wanted to marry him. King Baldwin finally gave his consent and made Guy his regent. But Guy soon angered the king, who summoned his vassals and transfered the regency to Raymond III. As a precaution he named Baldwin V as heir. He disinherited Sibylla and Guy and immediately celebrated the marriage of his other sister, Isabella, to Humphrey IV of Toron, an eminent member of the local nobility. Finally, he summoned Guy to appear before the high court and, when Guy refused to open the doors of Ashkelon, where he had taken refuge, the king ordered the confiscation of his belongings. Thus, if Baldwin V were to die, Raymond III would remain regent until the pope, the emperor, and the western kings decided on the successor. The party of the old nobility had won.

In 1186 there was a reversal: A year after his uncle the king died, the young Baldwin V also died. Guy of Lusignan outmaneuvered Raymond III and had himself crowned king of Jerusalem after all. Humphrey and the Hospitalers did not want to start a civil war. Raymond III sequestered himself in Tiberias and made an agreement with Saladin. The division was complete.

Reginald of Châtillon married the widow of Raymond of Poitiers to become prince of Antioch in 1153. He immediately revealed his brutal nature in his treatment of Patriarch Aimery of Limoges (left), who had governed the principality before him. Accusing Aimery of conspiracy, Reginald had him imprisoned in a dungeon and whipped until he bled. Then the old man was covered with honey, tied up, and left naked in the desert, exposed to the sun and flies. Below: An Arab troop.

The Latin States Lost Their Unity

The Latin states needed peace and time to repair their unity, but Reginald of Châtillon broke the truce in 1187. Once more, he attacked and plundered a caravan coming from Mecca and again refused to return the spoils. Saladin could not put off dealing with him; Reginald was like a thorn deeply imbedded in the side of his empire. He affronted the emir's honor by taxing and plundering the caravans heading for Mecca or moving between Syria and Egypt; moreover, by cultivating relations with the Bedouin tribes of Transjordan, Reginald had developed an impressive intelligence network and had the means to divide Saladin's empire.

Saladin ran the considerable risk of losing face among his people and seeing a movement toward dismemberment start among his states if he did not retaliate. So he chose to fight. His empire, at the time, was at the height of its power, and the kingdom of Jerusalem was weakened and isolated, not only on an international level but also on a local level, since Antioch had made a truce with Saladin. The de facto secession of Reginald and Raymond III of Tripoli weakened it considerably.

Saladin Proclaimed the Jihad

The sultan mobilized all his forces—now some twelve thousand cavalry, a spectacle that had not been seen since the Franks arrived. To start with he had to besiege the fortresses of Moab and Montreal to neutralize Reginald of Châtillon. Meanwhile, Guy of Lusignan decided to mend relations with Raymond III. On Guy's order, representatives of the party of the nobility, accompanied by the grand masters of the two military orders, went to Raymond at Tiberias. A reconciliation was reached, but the distrust remained.

In June 1187 Saladin crossed the Jordan River with most of his troops and lay siege to Tiberias on 2 July. He placed a contingent on the plateau overlooking the city at the west to protect himself against a Frankish offensive. The

"The holy war and the passion it evoked had a very strong hold on his heart and his body; he spoke of nothing else, he thought of nothing but preparing for this war, he concerned himself with only those who would fight it, he found congenial only those who spoke of it or promoted participation in it."

Baha ad-Din, secretary to Saladin, in his *Sultanly Anecdotes*, 12th century

Franks marched toward Saffuriya, where they found abundant springs and took control of all the routes from Galilee. They had to make a choice: Should they stay to Saladin's rear and watch his movements, abandoning Tiberias to its fate, or go to Tiberias and force Saladin to lift the siege? Raymond III recommended prudence at first, even though his own family, trapped in Tiberias, risked falling into Saladin's hands. He advised that the troops prepare themselves for action but wait for the Islamic army to disperse, as had happened in 1183. The plateau that they occupied was arid and had only one water source. His counsel prevailed, but that very night Gerard of Ridefort, grand master of the Templars and Raymond's personal enemy, told the king that Raymond, through his own ambition, sought to dishonor the king.

"All that night the Christians remained in their armor and suffered great thirst. But the Saracens did not want to fight until the heat came.... Then the Saracens arrived and set fires all around them to cause them as much misery as possible, from the sun as well as the fire.... When the king observed the distress of our men and that the sergeants were deserting, he ordered the count of Tripoli to charge the Saracens."

William of Tyre

The Franks Were Crushed at Hattin in 1187

Already accused once of cowardice for not

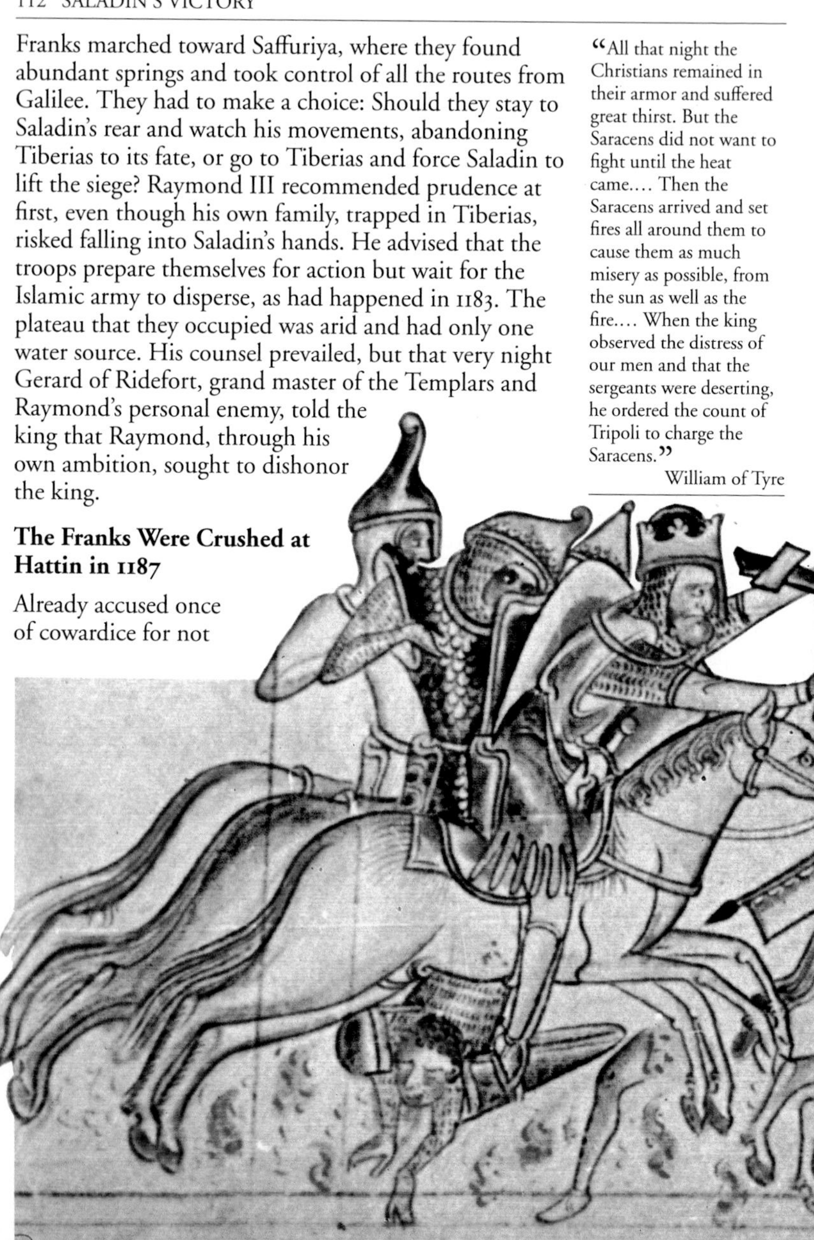

fighting Saladin in 1183, Guy of Lusignan felt he could not avoid battle this time. He ordered his army forward on 3 July. They marched on the plateau under the blazing sun. Saladin blocked access to the sole source of water with his sixty thousand men, and his mounted archers subjected the Franks to constant harassment. The Franks camped for the night and awoke the next morning to find themselves surrounded. Raymond III succeeded in breaking through the Muslim line, but the ranks closed in behind him, turning his feat into a strategic failure.

All the Franks were killed or captured. In one day Saladin had demolished the entire offensive power of the Franks. They still had the city ramparts and the fortified castles—but no one to man them. Back in Rome Pope Urban III died from shock when he heard the news.

"The Muslims captured their great cross, called the True Cross, which was said to contain a piece of wood from the one on which the Messiah had been crucified, according to them. This prize hit them very hard as it struck them as confirmation of death and disaster."

Ibn al-Athir

The capture of the True Cross is pictured at left, and a plan of battle from Saladin's manuals is shown above.

S.TAHSINE

This painting, by an Arab artist in 1954, represents the peace settlement of 2 September 1192 as the surrender of the Franks to Saladin: While Saladin sits straight on his throne, Richard I (the Lion-Heart), seated at his side, nods deferentially toward him and the Frankish soldiers throw their weapons at his feet. Actually, in his hurry to return to England, Richard I made a hasty peace but did not surrender. While Richard made it possible for the Franks to hold on, the victory undoubtedly belonged to Saladin. Of the former kingdom of Jerusalem, the Franks retained only the coastal zone from north of Tyre to south of Jaffa. The principality of Antioch and the Ismaili domain of the Djebel Ansariya Mountains were included for three and a half years in the peace treaty.

Saladin, Magnanimous in Victory, Took Jerusalem

The sultan treated Guy of Lusignan as a king and spared the prisoners but killed Reginald of Châtillon and declared the Templars and Hospitalers the sworn enemies of Islam. One by one, he lay siege to the cities and fortresses of the Franks, offering advantageous conditions to the inhabitants if they surrendered. The Franks of Jerusalem put up resistance, then warned Saladin that if he did not promise them their lives, they would leave no one alive, Frank or Muslim, and would burn all the mosques before dying in battle. Faced with the threat of the destruction of the mosque of Umar (the Dome of the Rock) and the death of all of Jerusalem's Muslims, Saladin agreed not to avenge the Franks for their massacre of 1099.

But the population had to pay a ransom: ten bezants per male, five per female. The poor were assessed at ten thousand bezants per seven thousand men. The patriarch and the bourgeois contributed to the ransom of the poor, but the military orders held onto their funds. Saladin and his brother even paid for many Christians themselves. In all, eight thousand were paid for collectively, ten thousand were set free by Saladin without payment, and ten to fifteen thousand were sold as slaves, of which five thousand went to Egypt to construct fortresses. On 2 October 1187 the citadel was taken. The church of the Holy Sepulcher was closed and all the mosques reopened. Of the kingdom of Jerusalem, only Tyre remained,

After Hattin, Guy of Lusignan, set free by Saladin, lay siege to Acre. His forces were considerably inferior to those of the besieged, but just in time, the first contingents of the Third Crusade showed up. The siege wore on. A split developed among the Franks between supporters of Guy of Lusignan and those of Conrad of Montferrat. The rest of the crusaders finally arrived, the French under Philip Augustus and the English under Richard the Lion-Heart. After eleven months, the Franks captured the city. The siege and the capture of Acre are shown above; Frederick I (Barbarossa) is depicted opposite, below.

valiantly defended by Conrad of Montferrat. Tripoli and Antioch were now on their own.

"If Allah had not deigned to show his benevolence toward the Muslims by having the king of the Germans perish...today we would be writing: Syria and Egypt formerly belonged to Islam."
Ibn al-Athir

Saladin's Victory Evoked a Strong Response in the West: The Third Crusade

Western Christianity had changed over the course of a century. The crusades were no longer a French-led enterprise. The king of England and the German emperor now joined, along with small contingents of Normans, Danes, Frisians, Saxons, and Flemish. Rapidly regrouped by Guy of Lusignan, they lay siege to Acre. In 1188 Emperor Frederick I Barbarossa of Germany took the land route to the East. He achieved a major victory in Anatolia over the sultan of Iconium but drowned while crossing the Saleph River in Cilicia. In 1190 Philip Augustus of France and Richard I (the Lion-Heart) of England took the sea route. Blown off course on the way, Richard captured Cyprus, which would come to serve as a solid base for the crusaders. Together, they helped Guy bring about the capitulation of Acre in July 1191.

While Philip Augustus went back to France, Richard

the Lion-Heart addressed himself to the problem of the succession to the throne of Jerusalem. The claim of Guy of Lusignan, whose wife, Sibylla, had died, was recognized. Conrad of Montferrat, who had defended Tyre and married Isabella, Baldwin IV's sister, was to succeed him.

Richard headed a strong army, large, well-trained, and equipped with reliable war machines. He carried off victories at Arsuf on 14 September 1191 and at Jaffa in August 1192. But he could not go too far from the sea, where his supplies came from, and had to halt his advance less than eight miles from Jerusalem.

Saladin was unable to repeat his successful mobilization of the Islamic world in 1187. With only his own army at his disposal, he agreed to a truce on 2 September 1192. The next year he died.

The Third Crusade Preserved the Very Existence of the Latin States

The Franks retained control of the coast from Tyre to Jaffa. Freedom for pilgrims, whether Christians bound for Jerusalem or Muslims for Mecca, was guaranteed. The Third Crusade had narrowed the scope of Saladin's triumph, forcing him to leave in place a Frankish state, limited as it was. It demonstrated the military might of

When he found it useful Saladin resorted to the execution of prisoners.

the West and its ability to send a powerful military contingent overseas. Finally, it also revealed the West's readiness to mobilize for the Holy Land.

Nonetheless, Saladin's victories remain impressive. The attempt by the kingdom of Jerusalem and the other Latin states to found a Frankish nation in the East had clearly failed, and the notion of retaking Jerusalem by force seemed to be out of the question.

Richard the Lion-Heart won his enemies' respect through his extravagant bravery, and that of his troops (below, he is shown on a turret in Jaffa, holding out against Saladin's attacks), rather than through the nobility of his soul. Indeed, the English king demonstrated a capacity for cruelty and brutality that called to mind Reginald of Châtillon. After the capture of Acre in August 1191, impatient with the slow pace of negotiations with Saladin and no doubt wary of being tricked, he led his Muslim prisoners (from 2,700 to 3,000, according to chroniclers) out of the city and then, while the prisoners next in line watched, had their throats cut (left).

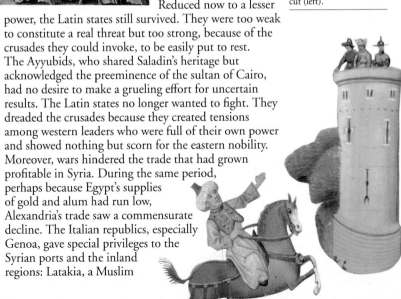

The Latin States Struggled On

Reduced now to a lesser power, the Latin states still survived. They were too weak to constitute a real threat but too strong, because of the crusades they could invoke, to be easily put to rest. The Ayyubids, who shared Saladin's heritage but acknowledged the preeminence of the sultan of Cairo, had no desire to make a grueling effort for uncertain results. The Latin states no longer wanted to fight. They dreaded the crusades because they created tensions among western leaders who were full of their own power and showed nothing but scorn for the eastern nobility. Moreover, wars hindered the trade that had grown profitable in Syria. During the same period, perhaps because Egypt's supplies of gold and alum had run low, Alexandria's trade saw a commensurate decline. The Italian republics, especially Genoa, gave special privileges to the Syrian ports and the inland regions: Latakia, a Muslim port (which exempted them from paying customs duty twice), as well as Acre and other Frankish ports, all possible refuges in case of war.

The Fourth Crusade Was Diverted and Ended with the Capture of Constantinople

The papacy persisted in its appeals to a holy war, and a fourth crusade was prepared. However, it was diverted under complex circumstances. Since the end of the 11th century the Italian republics had obtained exorbitant commercial licenses in Byzantium—as elsewhere in the East. But in 1182, in a violent anti-Latin pogrom, the people of Constantinople massacred all the Latins living in the city, including many Italians. According to some theories, as payment for Venetian sea transport to the Holy Land, the crusaders agreed to make a detour to Constantinople to help the Venetians exact revenge and re-establish their economic status. Because of dynastic divisions that raged throughout the empire, the crusaders ended up attacking the city.

They captured it, pillaged it, and founded an Eastern Latin Empire there, while the Greeks established a Byzantine Empire in exile at Nicaea.

The Fifth Crusade (1217–21) unfolded in Egypt. The Franks hoped to obtain Jerusalem in exchange for planned

From the Christian point of view, the Fourth Crusade was an unmitigated scandal. Aimed at the infidels, it resulted in the capture of Constantinople, the greatest Christian capital of the period. The crusaders besieged the city a first time to install Alexius IV on the throne. On 12 April 1204, to put an end to the national resistance led by Alexius Ducas, they captured it again, this time by sea (below). The Byzantine Empire never recovered from the blow. It might be expected that the prize of Constantinople would have propped up the Latin states of the East. The opposite proved to be true, for in order to hold onto it, the westerners had to divide their forces.

conquests in what had become the heart of the Ayyubid Empire. They carried off important victories. The Ayyubids proposed the restoration of the kingdom of Jerusalem, within its former borders. But the pope's legate, in charge of the expedition, rejected this proposal, aiming instead for the creation of a Frankish state in Egypt. The expedition ended disastrously.

Jerusalem, holy to three different faiths: above, the Tower of David, the Dome of the Rock, and the Holy Sepulcher.

Jerusalem Returned to the Christians

In the second quarter of the 13th century, the international outlook changed once again. The Muslim state of Khwarezm, to the east of the Caspian Sea, was crushed by the Mongols led by Genghis Khan. It was doubtlessly the threat of the Mongols that explains the success of the crusade led by the German Emperor Frederick II. It had created a furor because Frederick II had been excommunicated before leaving for the Holy Land due to his conflicts with the pope.

In addition, Frederick II succeeded through negotiations and mutual agreements with the "heathens" and not by means of war. The treaty of Jaffa, negotiated in February 1229 with Sultan al-Kamil, delivered the city

of Jerusalem to Frederick II, king of Jerusalem, under conditions that satisfied Islam but not the papacy: The mosques of Umar (the Dome of the Rock) and of al-Aqsa remained with the Muslims, while the church of the Holy Sepulcher reverted to the Christians. The treaty was to be in effect for ten years, five months, and forty days, but by 1244, the successors of al-Kamil fought among themselves and, reinforced by the fugitives from Khwarezm, retook Jerusalem.

Louis did not pass up any opportunity to convert the infidels to Christianity. He warned his men to take care to avoid any massacres and to spare the women and children. He is shown above and below in the Holy Land, and, opposite below, taken prisoner in Egypt.

The Recapture of Jerusalem by Islam Unleashed the First Crusade of Saint Louis—or the Seventh Crusade

Pope Innocent IV commanded another crusade, the seventh, which lasted from 1248 to 1250, under the direction of King Louis IX (Saint Louis), who wished to fulfill an old vow. At this time, the German Empire and England were paralyzed. This crusade, which mobilized close to three thousand knights, could have posed a serious threat to Islam.

It turned out to be a complete

failure. The king and his knights disembarked at Damietta and were captured at Al-Mansura, in Egypt, on 6 April 1250. In return for a ransom of 400,000 bezants, they were set free. Meanwhile the Mamluks, Turkish slaves who had become the sultans' elite corps of soldiers, took power and established a military regime.

Saint Louis spent four years in the Holy Land, from 1250 to 1254, strengthening the fortresses and trying to reestablish unity among the Latin states. The states managed to survive only because of the power struggles between the Ayyubids of Syria and the Mamluks of Cairo.

"You are not unaware that I am the leader of the Christian community; in the same token, I recognize you as the leader of the Muslim community.... If I capture your land, it is a gift that falls in my hands; if they remain yours through victory, you can exert all your power on me. I have informed you and warned you of the armies under my control that swarm over mountain and plain, as plentiful as the pebbles in the earth; they are launched toward you with the swords of destiny."

Letter from Saint Louis to the sultan of Egypt

While it was rich in acts of bravery and even heroism, carefully prepared from a moral as well as a technical point of view, Saint Louis's campaign in Egypt (opposite and left), erred in its very conception, according to some contemporaries. These critics were opposed to a crusade that led to the conquest of an infidel country, even with the goal of extending the domain of Christ: "We believe that God was offended because the Christians should not venture overseas with any purpose beyond recovering Christ's heritage." The policy of the king of France seemed aimed more at the conquest of Egypt than at redeeming the pledge to recover the Holy Land. It is entirely possible that Saint Louis saw such a conquest primarily as a way to ensure the conversion of the Egyptians to Christianity.

The Mamluks Stopped the Mongols...

It was around this time that the Mongols came forward in strength—their size was astounding. Hulegu established a state in Iran and tried to conquer Mesopotamia and Syria. He took Baghdad and overthrew the Abbasid caliphate in 1258. The Latin states were wracked once again by internal divisions: Genoese against Venetians, then against Pisans; Philip of Monfort against the count of Jaffa; not to mention the ongoing dynastic disputes. Faced with the Mongolian threat the Franks became friendly with the Mamluks, who stopped the Mongols at Ayn Jalut in 1260. The Mamluk sultan of Cairo, Baybars, took over Muslim Syria and the Latin settlements in the interior and penned the Franks into a few sites on the coast. The Eighth Crusade, led by Saint Louis, came to nothing, as the king disembarked at Tunisia in 1270 and died there.

...and Expelled the Franks in 1291

Once more Syria and Egypt were united. In 1281 a new Mongolian invasion began. Since 1260 some Franks had envisioned an alliance with the Mongols. The Mamluks responded with force. After the victory at Homs, Sultan Qala'un decided to deal with the Latin states once and for all. Acre was taken on 18 May 1291 and its citadel, held by the Templars, fell on 28 May.

The Franks were driven out, with no hope of returning to Syria. A king of Jerusalem still existed, but his reign was confined to Cyprus. Thus ended an epoch encompassing two hundred years dominated by bold and powerful personalities whose least equivocal legacy was to have engendered mutual hostility, mistrust, and misunderstanding that have endured to this day.

Victorious over the Franks at Al-Mansura in 1250, the leaders of a Mamluk contingent (the Turkish slaves who formed the armies of Ayyubid Egypt) deposed their Ayyubid sultan and established an oligarchy. However, the true founder of the Mamluk regime was Baybars (1260–77), who fought against Mongols and Franks (opposite, Mamluk princes). After crushing the Mongols at Ayn Jalut in 1260, then at Homs in 1261, the Mamluks systematically eliminated the Franks while taking military precautions to protect them from a new crusade. It was Baybars's third successor who captured Acre on 18 May 1291. After that, the Frankish towns and castles surrendered without giving contest. On 14 August, even the Templars left Pilgrim Castle—the last Frankish castle on the seacoast—without a fight.

Left: The capture of Tripoli by the sultan of Egypt in 1288. Overleaf: 19th-century painting of a returning crusader.

DOCUMENTS

The First Crusade

The events of the First Crusade are known through numerous western, Byzantine, and eastern texts. All describe the remarkable success of a movement that the East completely failed to understand and that took everyone by surprise.

Pope Urban II preaching at Clermont before the king of France, Philip I.

Pope Urban II's Initial Call for a Crusade in 1095

The French priest Fulcher of Chartres wrote an account of Pope Urban II's speech at the Council of Clermont on 27 November 1095.

For you must hasten to carry aid to your brethren dwelling in the East, who need your help for which they have often entreated.

For the Turks, a Persian people, have attacked them, as many of you already know, and have advanced as far into Roman territory as that part of the Mediterranean which is called the Arm of Saint George [the Bosporus and the Sea of Marmara]. They have seized more and more of the lands of the Christians, have already defeated them

in seven times as many battles, killed or captured many people, have destroyed churches, and have devastated the kingdom of God. If you allow them to continue much longer they will conquer God's faithful people much more extensively.

Wherefore with earnest prayer I, not I, but God exhorts you as heralds of Christ to repeatedly urge men of all ranks whatsoever, knights as well as foot-soldiers, rich and poor, to hasten to exterminate this vile race from our lands and to aid the Christian inhabitants in time.

I address those present; I proclaim it to those absent; moreover Christ commands it. For all those going thither there will be remission of sins if they come to the end of this fettered life while marching by land, crossing by sea, or in fighting the pagans. This I grant to all who go, through the power vested in me by God.

Oh what a disgrace if a race so despicable, degenerate, and enslaved by demons should thus overcome a people endowed with faith in Almighty God and resplendent in the name of Christ! Oh what reproaches will be charged against you by the Lord Himself if you have not helped those who are counted like yourselves of the Christian faith!

Let those...who are accustomed to wantonly wage private war against the faithful march upon the infidels in a war which should be begun now and be finished in victory. Let those who have long been robbers now be soldiers of Christ. Let those who once fought against brothers and relatives now rightfully fight against the barbarians. Let those who have been hirelings for a few pieces of silver now attain an eternal reward. Let those who have been exhausting themselves to the detriment of body and soul now labor for a double glory. Yea on the one hand will be the sad and the poor, on the other the joyous and the wealthy; here the enemies of the Lord, there His friends.

Let nothing delay those who are going to go. Let them settle their affairs, collect money, and when winter has ended and spring has come, zealously undertake the journey under the guidance of the Lord.

Fulcher of Chartres
A History of the Expedition to Jerusalem: 1095–1127, Book I, Chapter III
trans. Frances Rita Ryan, 1969

The First Crusade from the Byzantine Perspective

Anna Comnena wrote The Alexiad, *a biography of her father, Emperor Alexius I Comnenus. In it, she describes the Franks' journey to Constantinople.*

[Alexius] had no time to relax before he heard a rumor that countless Frankish armies were approaching.... What actually happened was much more far-reaching and terrible than rumor suggested, for the whole of the West and all the barbarians who lived between the Adriatic and the Straits of Gibraltar migrated in a body to Asia, marching across Europe country by country with all their households. The reason for this mass-movement is to be found more or less in the following events. A certain Celt, called Peter, with the surname Koukoupetros [the Hermit], left to worship at the Holy Sepulcher and after suffering much ill-treatment at the hands of the Turks and Saracens who were plundering the whole of Asia, he returned home with difficulty. Unable to admit defeat, he wanted to make a second attempt by the same route, but realizing the folly of trying to do this alone (worse things might happen to him), he worked out a clever scheme. He decided to preach in all the Latin countries. A divine voice, he said, commanded him to proclaim to all the counts in France that all should depart from their homes, set out to worship at the Holy Shrine and with all their soul and might strive to liberate Jerusalem from the Agarenes [the Turks]. Surprisingly, he was successful. It was as if he had inspired every heart with some divine oracle. Celts assembled from all parts, one after another, with arms and horses and all the other equipment for war. Full of enthusiasm and ardor they thronged every highway, and with these warriors came a host of civilians, outnumbering the sand of the seashore or the stars of heaven, carrying palms and bearing crosses on their shoulders. There were women and children, too, who had left their own countries.

Anna Comnena
The Alexiad of Anna Comnena, Book X
trans. E. R. A. Sewter
1969

The First Crusade According to the 13th-Century Muslim Historian Ibn al-Athir

In 490 [the year 1097] the Franks attacked Syria. This is how it all began: Baldwin, their King, a kinsman of Roger the Frank, who had conquered Sicily, assembled a great army and sent word to Roger saying: "… Now I am on my way to you, to use your bases for my conquest of the African coast. Thus you and I shall become neighbors."

Roger called together his companions and consulted them about these proposals. "This will be a fine thing both for them and for us!" they declared, "for by this means these lands will be converted to the Faith!" At this Roger raised one leg and farted loudly, and swore that it was of more use than their advice. "Why?" "Because if this army comes here it will need quantities of provisions and fleets of ships to transport it to Africa, as well as reinforcements from my own troops. Then, if the Franks succeed in conquering this territory they will take it over and will need provisioning from Sicily. This will cost me my annual profit from the harvest. If they fail they will return here and be an embarrassment to me here in my own domain. As well as all this Tamim [emir of Tunisia] will say that I have broken faith with him and violated our treaty, and friendly relations and communications between us will be disrupted. As far as we are concerned, Africa is always there. When we are strong enough we will take it."

He summoned Baldwin's messenger and said to him: "If you have decided to make war on the Muslims your best course will be to free Jerusalem from their rule and thereby win great honor. I am bound by certain promises and treaties of allegiance with the rulers of Africa." So the Franks made ready and set out to attack Syria.

Another story is that the Fatimids of Egypt were afraid when they saw the Seljuks extending their empire through Syria as far as Gaza, until they reached the Egyptian border and Atsiz invaded Egypt itself. They therefore sent to invite the Franks to invade Syria and so protect Egypt from the Muslims. But God knows best.

Ibn al-Athir
Kamil at-Tawarikh
(*The Perfect History*), Book X, 185–8,

The four leaders of the First Crusade: Godfrey of Bouillon, Raymond IV of Toulouse, Bohemond of Taranto, and Tancred of Hauteville.

in *Arab Historians of the Crusades*, trans. from the Arabic by Francesco Gabrieli; trans. from the Italian by E. J. Costello, 1969

The Only Existing Native Eyewitness Account of the Capture of Antioch

This account by the Armenian monk John Hovannes, which appears at the end of a manuscript he copied at the monastery of Saint Barlaam in the town above Antioch, was written during the military operations of 1098.

That year the Lord visited his people, as it is written: "I will never leave thee, nor forsake thee." The all-powerful arm of God became their guide. They carried the sign of Christ's Cross, and having come over across the sea, massacred a multitude of infidels and caused many others to flee. They captured the town

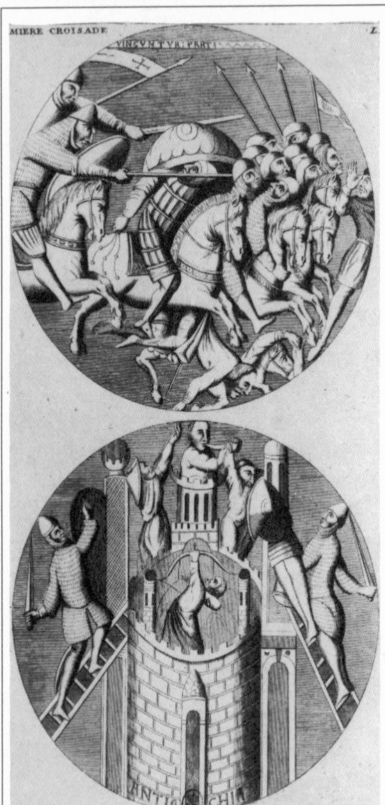

The capture of Antioch.

of Nicaea, to which they laid siege for five months. Then they came to our country, in the regions of Cilicia and Syria, and laid siege to Antioch, by surrounding the city.

For nine months they subjected themselves and the neighboring areas to severe trials. Finally, since the capture of such a strongly fortified site was not in the power of men, all-powerful God in his wisdom had mercy on and granted them success. They took the city and with the edge of their sword slew the arrogant dragon with its troops. And after one or two days, a great crowd came to the aid of their fellow [Muslims]; owing to their large numbers, they were scornful of the small force of the others, they assumed the insolence of their Pharaoh, hurling at them this phrase: "I shall kill them with my sword; my hand will prevail over them."

For fifteen days, reduced to the greatest anguish, they [the crusaders] were overwhelmed by distress, as they did not have sufficient food to sustain the lives of men and horses. And, seriously debilitated and frightened by the multitude of infidels, they gathered in the large basilica dedicated to the apostle Saint Peter, and with a great outcry and a river of tears created the effect of a flagellation of voices. They asked themselves something like, "Our Lord and Savior Jesus Christ, in whom we place our faith and by whose name we are called Christians in this city, you have brought us to this place. If we have sinned against you, you have many means with which to punish us. We beseech you not to let us fall into the hands of the infidels, so that they will not say to us when they are swollen with pride, "Where is your God?" And struck with the grace of the prayer, they encouraged one another, saying, "The Lord will lend strength to his people; the Lord will bless his people with peace." And each of them leapt onto his horse, they then threw themselves on the enemy; they scattered them, set them in flight, and massacred them until nightfall. That was a great joy for the Christians, and they enjoyed an abundance of wheat and barley, as in the time of Elisha before the gates of Samaria. For this reason they applied themselves to the prophetic hymn, "I praise you, Lord, for you have watched over me, and for my sake you did not bring joy to my enemy."

Based on Father Peeters's trans. of the original text from Armenian into Latin, in *Miscellanea Historica Alberti di Meyer*

The Capture of Maarat an-Numan

The western (Gesta Francorum) *and eastern (Ibn al-Athir) accounts of the events at Maarat an-Numan converge, but only the* Gesta Francorum *mentions acts of cannibalism.*

All this took place on Saturday, at vespers, at sunset, 11 December. Bohemond told the Saracen leaders through an interpreter to bring their wives and children, with their goods, to a palace above the gate and then he would undertake to save them from death.

Then our men entered the city, and whatever they came upon of any value in the houses or hiding places, each of them helped himself. As day broke, whenever they encountered the enemy, man or woman, they killed them. In all the city, there was no place empty of Saracen bodies, and it was nearly impossible to walk in the streets of the city without stepping on corpses. Bohemond apprehended those he had ordered to enter the palace, took from them all their goods, gold, silver, and other fine things, had some of them killed and had the others brought to Antioch to be sold.

The Franks stayed in this city for a month and four days, during which time the bishop of Orange died. Among our men were some who did not find there enough to satisfy their needs; this was caused as much by the length of their stay as the problem in finding food, as they could no longer find anything to eat. So they cut up the corpses, as bezants [coins] were discovered in their bellies; others cut off the flesh in pieces and cooked it in order to eat them.

Gesta Francorum et Aliorum Hierosolymitanorum

The Franks Seize Maarat an-Numan

After dealing this blow to the Muslims [at Antioch] the Franks marched on Maarat an-Numan and besieged it. The inhabitants valiantly defended their city. When the Franks realized the fierce determination and devotion of the defenders they built a wooden tower as high as the city wall and fought from the top of it, but failed to do the Muslims any serious harm. One night a few Muslims were seized with panic and in their demoralized state thought that if they barricaded themselves into one of the town's largest buildings they would be in a better position to defend themselves, so they climbed down from the wall and abandoned the position they were defending. Others saw them and followed their example, leaving another stretch of wall undefended, and gradually, as one group followed another, the whole wall was left unprotected and the Franks scaled it with ladders. Their appearance in the city terrified the Muslims, who shut themselves up in their houses. For three days the slaughter never stopped; the Franks killed more than 100,000 men and took innumerable prisoners.

Ibn al-Athir
Kamil at-Tawarikh, Book X, 190
in *Arab Historians of the Crusades*,
trans. from the Arabic by Francesco Gabrieli; trans. from the Italian by E. J. Costello, 1969

The Taking of Jerusalem

Jerusalem, the holy city of the Jews, Christians, and Muslims, was captured by the crusaders in 1099 and by Saladin in 1187, under very different circumstances.

The capture of the Holy City.

The Crusaders Capture Jerusalem

We attacked the city from all sides, day and night, on Wednesday and Thursday. But before we attacked the city, the bishops and priests, by preaching and exhortation, ordered everyone to hold a procession in honor of God all around the city and arranged for prayers, almsgiving, and fasting.

At dawn on Friday we attacked the city from all sides without being able to make any headway. We were all trembling and stunned. At the approach of the hour at which our Lord Jesus Christ deigned to suffer on the cross for us, our knights in the tower, namely Duke Godfrey and his brother, Count Eustace, made a fierce attack. Then one of our knights, named Lethold, climbed over the city wall. As soon as he ascended, all the city's defenders fled from the wall. Our men followed, killing and beheading them all the way to the Temple of Solomon. There was such slaughter there that our men waded in blood up to their ankles....

The emir who was in the Tower of David surrendered to the Count and opened to him the gate where pilgrims used to pay the tribute. Our pilgrims, on entering the city, pursued and slaughtered the Saracens all the way to the Temple of Solomon, where the Turks were gathered. The enemy fought most vigorously for a whole day and their blood flowed through the Temple. Finally the pagans were overcome. Our men captured a number of men and women in the Temple. The captives were either killed or allowed to live, as our men saw fit. On the roof of Solomon's Temple there was a very large gathering of pagans of both sexes. To these people Tancred and Gaston of Bearn had given their banners. Soon our

The attack on Jerusalem in 1099.

men were running all around the city, seizing gold and silver, horses and mules, and houses filled with all kinds of goods.

Rejoicing and weeping for joy, our people came to the sepulcher of Jesus our Savior to worship and pay their debt. At dawn our men cautiously went up to the roof of the Temple and attacked the Saracen men and women, beheading them with naked swords. Some of the Saracens, however, leaped from the Temple roof. Tancred, seeing this, was greatly angered.

Our men then took counsel and decided that everyone should pray and give alms so that God might choose for them whomever he pleased to rule over the others and govern the city. They ordered that all the dead Saracens should be cast out of the city because of the great stench, since the city was filled with their corpses. The living Saracens dragged the dead outside the gates and made heaps of them, as large as houses. No one ever saw or heard of such slaughter of pagan peoples, for funeral pyres were formed of them like pyramids and no one knows their numbers save God alone.

Gesta Francorum et Aliorum Hierosolymitanorum
trans. James A. Brundage, in Brundage, *Crusades: A Documentary Survey*, 1962

Part of a Letter Written by a Jew the Day Following the Capture of Jerusalem by the Crusaders

You may remember, my Lord, that many years ago I left our country to seek God's mercy and help in my poverty, to behold Jerusalem and return thereupon. However, when I was in Alexandria God brought about circumstances which caused a slight delay.... The sea grew stormy.... Moreover, mutinies [spread throughout the country and reached] even Alexandria, so that we ourselves were besieged several times and the city was ruined.... The end however was good, for the Sultan—may God bestow glory upon his victories—conquered the city and caused justice to abound in it in a manner unprecedented in the history of any king in the world; not even a dirham [coin of very small value] was looted from anyone. Thus I had come to hope that because of his justice and strength God would give the land into his hands, and I should thereupon go to Jerusalem in safety and tranquillity. For this reason I proceeded from Alexandria to Cairo, in order to start [my journey] from there.

When, however, God had given Jerusalem, the blessed, into his hands this state of affairs continued for too short a time to allow for making a journey there. The Franks arrived and killed everybody in the city, whether of Ishmael or Israel; and the few who survived the slaughter were made prisoners. Some of these have been ransomed since, while others are still in captivity in all parts of the world.

Now, all of us had anticipated that our Sultan—may God bestow glory upon his victories—would set out against them [the Franks] with his troops and chase them away. But time after time our hope failed.

"Contemporary Letters on the Capture of Jerusalem by the Crusaders"
Journal of Jewish Studies 3, no. 4,
trans. S. D. Goitein, 1952

The Taking of Jerusalem Recounted by an Arab Historian

After their vain attempt to take Acre by siege, the Franks moved on to Jerusalem and besieged it for more than six weeks. They built two towers, one of which, near Sion, the Muslims burnt down, killing everyone inside it. It had scarcely ceased to burn before a messenger arrived to ask for help and to bring the news that the other side of the city had fallen. In fact Jerusalem was taken from the north on the morning of Friday 22 shaban 492 [15 July 1099]. The population was put to the sword by the Franks, who pillaged the area for a week. A band of Muslims barricaded themselves into the Oratory [Tower] of David and fought on for several days. They were granted their lives in return for surrendering. The Franks honored their word, and the group left by night for Ascalon. In the Masjid [Mosque] al-Aqsa the Franks slaughtered more than 70,000 people, among them a large number of Imams and Muslim scholars, devout and ascetic men who had left their homelands to live lives of pious seclusion in the Holy Place. The Franks stripped the Dome of the Rock of more than forty silver candelabra, each of them weighing 3,600 drams [14 pounds], and a great silver lamp… as well as a hundred and fifty smaller silver candelabra and more than twenty gold ones, and a great deal more booty. Refugees from Syria reached Baghdad in ramadan, among them the qadi Abu Sad al-Harawi. They told the Caliph's ministers a story that wrung their hearts and brought tears to their eyes. On Friday they went to the Cathedral Mosque and begged for help, weeping so that their hearers wept with them as they described the sufferings of the Muslims in that Holy City: the men killed, the women and children taken prisoner, the homes pillaged. Because of the terrible hardships they had suffered, they were allowed to break the fast.

Ibn al-Athir
Kamil at-Tawarikh, Book X, 193–5
in *Arab Historians of the Crusades*
trans. from the Arabic by Francesco Gabrieli; trans. from the Italian by E. J. Costello, 1969

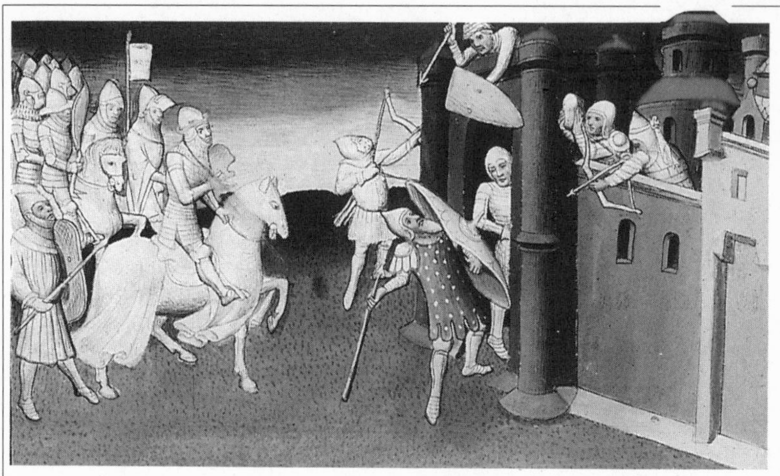

Saladin retakes Jerusalem in 1187.

Saladin Retakes Jerusalem, According to His Secretary, Imad ad-Din

On Friday 20 rajab [25 September] the Sultan moved to the northern side and pitched his tent there, cutting the Frankish lines and opening up the way to death. He mounted the catapults, and by this means milked the udders of slaughter, making the Rock groan under the impact of missiles; his reward was the hosts of evil behind the wall. They could no longer put a head outside the gates without meeting death and the day of disaster, and casting their souls into perdition. The Templars clamored, the barons leapt to their destruction in Hell, the Hospitalers went to damnation, the "Brethren" found no escape from death. No band of soldiers cast itself between the stones from the catapults and their objective; in every heart on either side burned the fire of longing, faces were exposed to the blade's kiss, hearts were tormented with longing for combat, hands cleaved to the hilts of their bloody swords, minds were intent upon finding those whose spirit was slow to devote itself fully to the cause. The bases of the walls and the teeth of their battlements were battered and broken down by stones from the catapults' slings.... How many boulders came down out of heaven upon them, how many blocks of sandstone plunged into the earth, how many blazing firebrands bespattered them! The damage caused by the catapults, the extraordinary extent of their devastation, the effects of their concentration, the whistling wind of their flight, the extent of their range were beyond compare.... The enemies ordnance was smashed and broken, the moat crossed and the attack sustained. The victory of Islam was clear, and so was the death of Unbelief [the non-believers].... The enemy feared that it would be crushed, its strong morale gave way to distress. The city became Muslim and the infidel belt around it was cut. Ibn Barzan came out to secure a treaty with the Sultan, and asked for an amnesty for his people. But the Sultan refused and upheld his claims, saying: "Neither amnesty nor mercy for you! Our only desire is to inflict perpetual subjection upon you; tomorrow will make us your masters by main force. We shall kill and capture you wholesale, spill men's blood and reduce the poor and women to slavery." He absolutely refused to grant them an amnesty, and their response was without bravura; they feared the consequences of a sudden decision, and communicated their fear. They said: "If we must despair of your mercy and fear your power and lose all hope of your magnanimity, and if we are sure that there is no escape or way out, no peace or safety, no grace or generosity, then we shall seek death, and shall fight like men who sell their lives dearly.... No one will be wounded before he has first wounded ten men himself, no one will shake hands with death before he has been seen to stave off destruction with open hands. We shall burn the houses and pull down the Dome, and leave to you to enjoy the grief of losing it; we shall kill every Muslim prisoner in our hands, and we have thousands, since it is well known that each one of us spurns dishonor and honors his reputation. As for our possessions, we shall destroy them rather than hand them over, and as for our sons, we shall be quick to slay them; you shall not find us slow to do it. What advantage do you gain from this ungenerous spirit of negation, you who would only lose everything by such a gain? What delusions are born of the hope of success, when only peace will repair the evil! How many men, forced to make a journey in the dark, have wandered from the path in the gloom of night before the dawn appeared!"

Then the Sultan called a council meeting and sent for the leaders of his victorious hosts, consulting with them on the question, discussing with them in secret and in the open. He begged them to reveal to him their innermost thoughts and to display their hidden opinions; he wanted to light the spark in them, he asked to know their minds, he beguiled them into pronouncing the best solution and conferred with them on the most profitable peace treaty.... So after repeated requests and consultations and messages and importunings and intercessions an amount was fixed that satisfied us and would act as weighty caution, for which they were to ransom themselves and their possessions and save their men, women, and children. Under the treaty, at the end of forty days, whoever was unable to pay what he owed or refused to pay it was to become our slave by right and come into our possession. The tax was ten dinar for each man, five for a woman, and two for a boy or girl. Ibn Barzan and the Patriarch and the Grand Masters of the Temple and the Hospital stood guarantee, and Ibn Barzan gave 30,000 dinar for the poor, fulfilling his word faithfully and without default.... Once the tax had been fixed they surrendered the city on Friday 27 rajab [2 October], surrendering it under duress like ill-gotten gains rather than a legitimate deposit. There were more than 100,000 persons in the city, men, women, and children. The gates were closed upon them all, and representatives appointed to make a census and demand the sum due. An emir or representative was appointed to each gate, to keep count of those coming and going; those who paid, went out, while those who did not settle their debt remained prisoners within.... There was great negligence and widespread peculation [embezzlement] and anyone who paid a bribe was allowed to get out, for the officials strayed from the path of honesty to accept bribes. Some people were let down from the walls on ropes, some carried out hidden in luggage, some changed their clothes and went dressed as Muslim soldiers....

The Franks began selling their possessions and taking their precious things out of safe-keeping to sell them for nothing in the market of abjection. People made bargains with them and bought the goods at very low prices.... The Grand Patriarch gathered up all that stood above the Sepulcher, the gold-plating and gold and silver artifacts, and collected together the contents of the church of the Resurrection, precious things of both metals and of the two sorts of fabric. Then I said to the Sultan: "These are great riches, their value is quite clearly 200,000 dinar; free exit is permitted to personal property but not to that of churches and convents; do not allow these rascals to keep this in their grasp." But he replied: "If we interpret the treaty to their disadvantage they will accuse us of breaking the faith and of being ignorant of the true essence of the thing. I prefer to make them obey the letter of the treaty, so that they are then unable to accuse the Believers of breaking their word, but will tell others of the benefits we have bestowed upon them." So they left the heavy objects and carried away the most precious and the lightest, and shook from their hands the dust of their heritage and the sweepings of their dung heap [the Holy Sepulcher].

When Jerusalem was purified of the filth of the hellish Franks and had stripped off her vile garments to put on the robe of honor, the Christians, after paying their tax, refused to leave, and asked to be allowed to stay on in safety, and gave prodigious service and worked for us with all their might, carrying out every task with discipline and cheerfulness. They paid "the tax for protection permitted to them, humbly." They stood ready to accept whatever might be inflicted on them, and their affliction grew as they stood waiting for it. Thus they became in effect tribute-payers, reliant upon [Muslim] protection; they were used and employed in menial tasks and in their position they accepted these tasks as if they were gifts.

Imad ad-Din
in *Arab Historians of the Crusades*,
trans. from the Arabic by Francesco Gabrieli; trans. from the Italian by E. J. Costello 1969

After retaking Jerusalem, Saladin made the crusaders file past him.

Hospitalers and Templars

The Hospitalers and the Templars represented the only permanent armed force of the Franks. It was composed of lay brethren who were also knights. They were responsible for keeping watch at most of the huge crusader fortresses—and, with their wealth, they were the only ones who had the means to maintain the large castles. The Hospitalers have remained faithful to their military vocation up to the present day, while the Templars, grown too powerful and rich, suffered a tragic fate under Philip IV, who succeeded in abolishing the order.

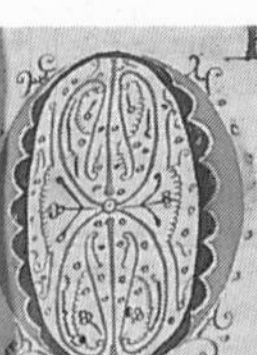

The Warrior Monks

The most original creation of the crusaders and of the crusades, the orders were the most sublime realization of the two great ideologies of medieval Europe—monastic life and knighthood—and became one of the most profound expressions of the ethos of the Middle Ages.

The idea behind the military orders did not generate among clerics or monks. Its initiators were laymen, and the orders were one of the earliest creative efforts of the noble class in the realm of ethics and ideology. Immediately after the crusaders captured Jerusalem, a Provençal knight named Gerald gathered a group of knights to care for the sick and wounded. The stench of cadavers strewn in the streets still filled the city when the small company of knights began its charitable work in an improvised hospital. The concept of a hospice and hospital were not new.… The innovation of the new institution was in fact that it was laymen—knights—not monks and nuns, who assumed the care of the sick, humble and needy.…

This voluntary association of idealists adopted the rules of monastic association, and its members took the triple vow of poverty, chastity, and obedience. For almost a generation it seemed that the order's future would be that of a monastic institution with Hospitaler aims.…

The order of the Templars—so called because its earliest abode was in the "Temple of Solomon" in Jerusalem (that is, in the mosque of al-Aqsa)

Rules of the order of the Templars.

—was built upon different premises which, in a sense, were far more congenial to the social class whose members joined its ranks. It was established by Hugh de Payns, who gathered a small group of knights in a voluntary association to serve as armed convoys for pilgrims on their way from Jerusalem to Jericho and thence to the traditional place of Jesus's baptism in the Jordan. The general state of insecurity during the first two decades of the kingdom's existence was not only due to poorly defended borders and insufficient fortifications. It was felt quite keenly within the borders of the kingdom as well, since the population of the countryside remained Muslim, and crusader authority extended only as far as the power to dominate the native population by force. The Muslims remained hostile.... Travel was extremely dangerous in the hilly and mountainous regions of Judea and Galilee, making a pilgrimage to Saint John's Ford, Bethlehem, or Nazareth a hazardous venture. The situation was no better on the main road from the port of Jaffa through the plain of Ramle to Jerusalem. To protect the pilgrims, the Templars organized military convoys which became part of crusader scenery.

This early military association soon evolved into a community of the pledged. Some rudimentary rules may already have been laid down by the founder in 1118 and were officially incorporated into the rules of the order when it received ecclesiastical sanction. The new association received moral backing from an outstanding spiritual authority of the period, Saint Bernard of Clairvaux....

The grand master of the Templars.

The new order met with tremendous success. It was favored by the local king and nobles because it fulfilled one of the kingdom's urgent needs; but its appeal was immediately felt throughout Christendom, and branches of the order were established in almost every country. The vow of poverty of the founding knights remained in force for the individual, but not for the collectivity. The white mantles and new crosses of the Templars soon symbolized power and wealth....

The emergence and the sensational success of the Templars had immediate repercussions within the older order of Saint John. Founded a generation earlier, it now had to compete with the strong appeal exercised by the Templars. The Hospitalers faced the challenge by adding military duties to their obligations, and soon black mantles and eight-pointed crosses would identify the military contingents of the order. They would become not just an integral part of the kingdom's army, but—together with contingents of other military orders—its very standing army. Whereas the feudal host had to be mobilized anew for every emergency, the military orders were an army of knights permanently on alert, always ready for action.

From the mid-1130s the two military orders not only supplied contingents to the kingdom's army but assumed the defense of key military positions. Fortified points, towers, and castles were handed over to the orders, and soon the whole network of roads and communications was policed by their patrols. Moreover, from the second half of the 12th century, with the growth of the Muslim threat, the orders implanted themselves in the huge castles which defended the borders of the kingdom and the northern crusader establishments.... The orders grew rich through grant and privilege. The Hospitalers allegedly possessed 18,000 manors in Europe. The Templars, hardly poorer, ironically became the great European bankers of the 13th century, vying with the banking houses of Italy and even with the Lombards and Cahorsins, the most notorious usurers of medieval Europe. On the one hand, the safety of

Right: Tomb effigy of a Templar.
Opposite: Seal of the Templars from 1255.

their well-guarded castles and towers, called "the Temples" for short, assured the security of the deposits, and their standing as members of the Church turned the order's property into asylums against lay intervention. On the other, the orders' many branches facilitated the transfer of obligations and credits from place to place without actually transporting money over dangerous roads and seas.... No wonder, then, that Europe simultaneously praised and blamed the orders. Praises were heaped upon their valor, military skill, and devotion to Christendom. But these were counter-balanced by trenchant criticism of their wealth, censure of their alleged greed, and condemnation of the rivalries which undermined the stability, and even the very existence, of the crusader kingdom.

Joshua Prawer
The World of the Crusaders, 1972

Hospitalers and Templars in Battle

In the battle of Arsuf between Richard the Lion-Heart of England and Saladin, the Templars demonstrated two of their most noted qualities: bravery and insubordination.

Having rid himself of the Muslim prisoners, at the end of August Richard led his men out against Saladin.... The Hospitalers, who took the main weight of the attack, were hard pressed, but the left of the Christian line was not turned, and after each Turkish charge the English bowmen reformed and took a heavy toll of the enemy horsemen, the arrows from their long bows penetrating the Muslims' light armor as though it were egg shell. The pace was too great to last, and as the day grew hotter the Turkish cavalry began to tire; but still Richard did not give the order to charge. One after another, his subordinate commanders begged him to do so, the Grand Master of the Temple returning again and again to implore him to give the word, and again and again Richard told him to wait. But there is a limit to human patience and restraint, and two knights of the Temple, who had reached that limit, took matters into their own hands; without waiting for the command from Richard, they charged the enemy on the spur of the moment, and immediately all the Templars galloped after them. Imagining that the order to charge must have been given, all the other knights on the field of battle moved forward to the attack, gathering speed in a cloud of dust. Seeing that he could not stop his men, Richard spurred his horse into a gallop and joined them, taking command at the center of the attack. The sheer weight and momentum of a thousand or more steel-clad knights, each with a lance almost the size of a telegraph pole, and each mounted on a huge, snorting steel-clad horse weighing more than a ton is difficult to recreate in the imagination, and it proved too much for the tired and frightened Muslims. Some simply fled before the avalanche of steel, bone, and sweat could crash into them, while those who stood firm were crushed and broken, and in a matter of minutes the Muslim army was in flight. The field was Richard's, and so was the day.

Antony Bridge
The Crusades
1980

Jihad and Holy War

While the First Crusade began, in theory, as a Christian "holy war," for many it became more a struggle for power and territory. For the Muslims, however, the reverse was true: What began as territorial expansion and defense turned into a jihad—or holy war.

Saint Bernard of Clairvaux Exhorts the People of England to Join the Second Crusade

Now is the acceptable time, now is the day of abundant salvation. The earth is shaken because the Lord of heaven is losing his land, the land in which he appeared to men, in which he lived amongst men for more than thirty years; the land made glorious by his miracles, holy by his blood; the land in which the flowers of his resurrection first blossomed. And now, for our sins, the enemy of the cross has begun to lift his sacrilegious head there, and to devastate with the sword that blessed land, that land of promise. Alas, if there should be none to withstand him, he will soon invade the very city of the living God, overturn the arsenal of our redemption, and defile the holy places which have been adorned by the blood of the Immaculate Lamb. They have cast their greedy eyes especially on the holy sanctuaries of our Christian religion....

What are you doing, you mighty men of valor? what are you doing, you servants of the cross? will you thus cast holy things to dogs, pearls before

Circular map of the Arab world (1193).

Louis VII at the feet of Saint Bernard.

swine?... I call blessed the generation that can seize an opportunity of such rich indulgence as this, blessed to be alive in this year of jubilee, this year of God's choice....

But now, O mighty soldiers, O men of war, you have a cause for which you can fight without danger to your souls; a cause in which to conquer glorious and for which to die is gain.

But to those of you who are merchants, men quick to seek a bargain, let me point out the advantages of this great opportunity. Do not miss them. Take up the sign of the cross and you will find indulgence for all sins which you humbly confess. The cost is small, the reward is great....

If the pagans were similarly subjugated to us then, in my opinion, we should wait for them rather than seek them out with swords. But as they have now begun to attack us, it is necessary for those of us who do not carry a sword in vain to repel them with force. It is an act of Christian piety both "to vanquish the proud" and also "to spare the subjected," especially those for whom we have a law and a promise, and whose flesh was shared by Christ, whose name be forever blessed.

Saint Bernard
trans. Bruno Scott James
in James A. Brundage
Crusades: A Documentary Survey
1962

Byzantium and the Concept of the Crusade

The very concept of the crusade was incomprehensible to a Byzantine; the empire's struggles against the Persians and Islamic world never took on the character of a holy war. Heraclius's Persian wars were never considered "crusades," but the West insisted on regarding them as such since the Middle Ages. At the end of the 10th century, when Nicephorus II Phocas was leading expeditions into northern Syria that his successor, John Tzimisces, extended into Palestine, the patriarch refused the emperor's request to honor as martyrs the soldiers who had fallen in combat against the infidels. Faithful to early Christianity, the Byzantine Church opposed the use of arms by laymen—Saint Basil's canon bars all those who "commit murder at war" from Communion for three years—and *a fortiori* [especially] by clergymen.

Cecile Morrisson
Les Croisades, 1984

Crusade vs. Jihad

The crusades were not a response to Islam's holy war. At the end of the 11th century, the jihad had lost its allure; only the Murabits, in the Sahara, and the Turkomans, on the eastern borders and in Asia Minor, still upheld it, under the form of the *ghazwa*. On the other hand, the Latin West had begun a phase of expansion, at the expense of Islam, in Sicily and Spain. At the level of doctrine, the situations reversed: when it was a crusade, the Catholic holy war could be waged only to defend and set free oppressed Christians and the Holy Land, even if conquests were justified. The jihad, by contrast, was an offensive war intended to conquer infidels and force them to accept the law of Islam. However, medieval Muslim society was less closed than that of the Christian West; it respected the existence of non-Muslim communities within its folds and awarded a special status to "People of the Book," Jewish and Christian alike, favoring them with hospitality and protection, following the *dhimma*, as long as they recognized the established authority and paid the *jizya*, the tax specific to them. The jihad, unlike the crusade, did not demand that the conquered choose between conversion and death, nor did it, like the crusader states, have intolerance built into its legal system.

Cecile Morrisson
Les Croisades
1984

Saladin's Appeal to a Holy War

We hope in God most high, to whom be praise, who leads the hearts of Muslims to calm what torments them and ruins their prosperity. As long as the seas bring reinforcements to the enemy and the land does not drive them off, our country will continue to suffer at their hands, and our hearts to be troubled by the sickness caused by the harm they do us. Where is the sense of honor of the Muslims, the pride of the believers, the zeal of the faithful? We shall never cease to be amazed at how the Unbelievers, for their part, have shown trust, and it is the Muslims who have been lacking in zeal. Not one of them has responded to the call, not one intervenes to straighten what is distorted; but observe how far the Franks have gone; what unity they have achieved, what aims they pursue, what help they have given, what sums of money they have borrowed and spent, what wealth they have collected and distributed and divided among them! There is not a king left in their lands or islands, not a lord or rich man who has not competed with his neighbors to produce more support, and rivaled his peers in strenuous military effort. In defense of their religion they consider it a small thing to spend life and soul, and they have kept their infidel brothers supplied with arms and champions for the war. And all they have done, and all their generosity, has been done purely out of zeal for Him they worship, in jealous defense of their Faith. Every Frank feels that once we have reconquered the [Syrian] coast, and the veil of their honor is torn off and destroyed, this country will slip from their grasp, and our hand will reach out toward their own countries. The Muslims, on the other hand, are weakened and demoralized. They have become negligent and lazy, the victims of unproductive stupefaction and completely lacking in enthusiasm. If, God forbid, Islam should draw rein, obscure her splendor, blunt her sword, there would be no one, East or West, far or near, who would blaze with zeal for God's religion or choose to come to the aid of truth against error. This is the moment to cast off lethargy, to summon from far and near all those men who have blood in their veins. But we are confident, thanks be to God, in the help that will come from Him, and entrust ourselves to Him in sincerity of purpose and deepest devotion. God willing, the Unbelievers shall perish and the faithful have a sure deliverance.

Abu Shama
Kitab ar-Raudatain (*The Book of the Two Gardens*) Book II, 148
in *Arab Historians of the Crusades*
trans. from the Arabic
by Francesco Gabrieli;
trans. from the Italian
by E. J. Costello
1969

The jihad: the warrior's duties included defending and spreading Islam.

Warfare or Military Science

Easterners and westerners had different conceptions of war. The former, including the Byzantines, considered it an art, the subject of treatises. The latter saw it as a test of courage above all, and they restricted themselves to observing its basic principles.

Common Sense and Military Discipline

The attack of the medieval horsemen, though it relied for its effect on the collective mass of the participants, was essentially an aggregate of many individual charges; it depended for its success on impact with an enemy who, in resisting, would be shattered by its weight. If the enemy, like the Turks, was able to remove himself from its path, then the Franks, their formation loosening as they advanced, were vulnerable to counter-attack. Nor, after their original charge, could they be any longer controlled by the commander. A squadron (*acies*) of knights was like a projectile in the hands of the commander. When directed against the enemy it could strike him only once, and therefore to succeed must strike and shatter him *uno impetu*, in a single attack. The elusive tactics of the Turks set the Franks the problem of timing

The Franks maintain their battle formation under attack.

the charge, which was their most powerful tactical weapon, so that it succeeded in making contact with the main body of the enemy. The Frankish charge was renowned and feared throughout the Middle East....

The maintenance of their formation was a problem which faced the Syrian Franks throughout the 12th century, not only to enable the commander to exercise control, but to counter [the] Turkish tactics.... The importance attached by the Franks to preserving the solidity and cohesion of their battle or marching order may be seen in William of Tyre's use of the phrase *agmen* or *aciem dissolvere.* Loss of formation by organized squadrons was the prelude, or even the symptom of defeat. To resist the Turk it was essential to prevent him from separating the Franks one from the other. In 1170 Amalric led a force to oppose Saladin's invasion of southern Palestine. The Muslims attempted to destroy the Franks, but they preserved themselves by the solidity of their array.

The need for the Franks to remain "*solidius inter se conglobati*" was even more necessary when they fought on the march than on the normal battlefield. Any gaps in the column enabled the Turks to single out some part of the Latin force for attack. This was discovered at heavy cost by the pilgrims led across Asia Minor by Louis VII of France in 1147. At one point the leader of the vanguard, Geoffrey de Rancogne, disregarded his orders and went too far ahead of the main body. As a result the Turks were able to develop a strong attack on those who followed, to throw the whole line of march into confusion and to inflict great losses. To prevent the recurrence of such a disaster the line of march was more thoroughly organized, with advance-, flank-, and rear-guards, in which archers on foot were given a prominent part. Thereafter, "*fiebat juxta preceptum processio.*"

In 1191 the Turks gained a similar success. On the day on which King Richard began his southward march from Acre, the column, for which advance- and rear-guards had been appointed, was attacked by part of Saladin's army. The line of march was widely spaced, and the Muslims were repulsed only with difficulty. The lesson was learnt, and the Christian army continued its progress in more solid order. That a force should be "*seré e rengié*" was the highest praise which Ambroise could bestow upon it. On two occasions he recorded with approval a battle order so solid that it was impossible to throw a plum or an apple into the ranks without hitting a man or horse.

The maintenance of close order in face of enemy provocation was an achievement for which historians have not given 12th-century commanders in Syria sufficient credit. To endure attack without striking back at the enemy demands severe restraint of normal human instincts, and in all ages soldiers have borne such a situation only with difficulty. To none was it more intolerable than the medieval knight, who in war was an individualist jealous of his personal prowess and honor.

R. C. Smail
Crusading Warfare (1097–1193)
1956

Muslim Fighting Style

The Egyptian light cavalry was more mobile than that of the crusaders, but in hand-to-hand fighting the Egyptians seldom won a battle, unless overwhelming numbers or a successful ambush or stratagem placed them at a marked advantage. Normally the tough nucleus of the caliph's army or that of his vizier (the Fatimid caliphs seldom left their palaces and harems) was composed of troops Mamluk in origin. These troops were better skilled and were usually loyal to their commander. Often the battle was decided by these elite troops, with their flight or success directly influencing the other regiments of the Egyptian army.

The situation was entirely different vis-à-vis the armies of Mesopotamia, Syria, and Persia, which sometimes joined in a war against the crusaders. In addition to Arab tribes which roamed Mesopotamia and Syria and the local city militia, the *askars*, the main strength of these armies was the Seljuk Turks. Though more than a hundred years has elapsed since they left their native lands in Central Asia to make their fortunes in the Near East, these former nomads never forgot their traditional technique of fighting, that is *à la turque*. The essential element in this type of warfare was the mounted archer. The style of warfare was ancient and is even described in the Bible: "A people cometh from the north.... They shall lay hold on bow and spear; they are cruel and have no mercy; their voice roareth like the sea and they ride upon horses, set in array as men for war against thee (Jeremiah 6, 22–3)." Lightly equipped and charging on swift but sturdy horses, the Turks presented a challenge to the crusader armies. Not only were they far more mobile than the heavily mailed western knights, but their concept of war and battle was entirely different.

The strength of the crusader armies lay in their heavy cavalry, whose charge mowed down everything on its path. ... The result of the battle was often decided during the first encounter, unless the opponent could move forward reinforcements or its flanks could close and attack the assaulting army. But the Turkish opponent was not very cooperative and seldom agreed to a pitched battle and putting up a closed front to be destroyed by the westerners. Not only was he mobile, but he had brought with him from the Mongolian steppes the deadly bow. The Turks did not enter into direct contact but would discharge a hail of arrows at a gallop from a distance of some eighty meters [262 feet], where the weapons of the westerners—lance and javelin, not to mention the sword—could not reach them. The arrows could hardly miss the great, solid mass of mounted knights. In a static position, the crusaders were simply sitting ducks. An attempt to attack a Muslim army was like chasing the wind; it simply disappeared beyond the horizon. The situation was no better when the crusader host was on the move. Time and again, the Muslim cavalry would appear out of nowhere, circle around the mobile crusade host, release its volley of arrows and vanish, only to reappear a short time later with its quivers replenished.

In these circumstances the safety of the crusader knight depended on his mail, helmet, and shield. The arrows did not easily pierce his helmet and shield or penetrate the chain-rings of the mail, unless they struck at some vulnerable point like the neck or face.… But this did not prevent the Muslims from shooting the horses out from under the mounted knights. A dismounted knight was no knight at all. Not only was his pride pricked, but his military effectiveness was reduced to nil.

Very soon the crusaders answered the Muslim challenge by partially adopting the type of fighting *à la turque*. But this was not easy. The crusaders, who were not very flexible in their ways, fell back on native talent, and created native regiments called *Turcoples* (sons of the Turks) that copied the Seljuk Turks in armament and techniques of fighting. Swift horses, light armor, quiver and bow were their main characteristics.…

Successful as the use of the *Turcople* regiments might have been, the crusaders also reacted to the Turkish challenge by inventing an original way of fighting based on the rehabilitation of the common archer. Two hundred years before the longbows of the Welshmen decided English battles against French knights, the crusaders introduced foot archers as an integral part of their hosts.… Lightly equipped with an iron or leather cap, jerkins, a wooden shield, pike, bow and arrows, the archers became the front-line fighters of the host. Marching before the contingents of mounted knights, at their flanks and rear, they were responsible for keeping the enemy at a respectable distance and preventing Seljuk mounted archers from using their weapons effectively.…

The ingenious use of the foot archer on the march and in battle depended on the preservation of disciplined order among the various formations. This was a difficult problem in every medieval army, with its unbridled nobles.… Yet it was discipline, at least in the sense of not breaking the ranks of archers, on which the safety of the whole host depended.

The enemy soon discovered the soft spot in the crusader formations. As far as possible, the Muslims evaded any head-on encounter with the crusaders, for the chances were that they would be swept away by the whirlwind of the heavy iron cavalry.… On the other hand, they maneuvered to strike a wedge and separate the foot archers from the crusader cavalry. Once separated, the crusader mounted knights were stripped of archer protection and thus a target for the arrows of Turkish cavalry.

Joshua Prawer
The World of the Crusaders
1972

The Muslims harassed the enemy to break their ranks.

Portrait of Saladin

In the Islamic world Saladin was not without his detractors. The caliph took exception to his power, and the supporters of the Zengids persisted in seeing him as a usurper. With the passage of time, however, he became a legendary figure whose example has inspired numerous contemporary Arab heads of state. The Franks, surprisingly, accorded him immediate respect. The eyewitness account of his secretary, Baha ad-Din, follows.

Saladin (opposite) burned his cannons and galleys before retreating with his army (below).

His Generosity

The Prophet said: "When the generous man stumbles God takes his hand," and many other *hadith* speak of generosity. Saladin's was too widespread to be recorded here and too well known to need mention: I shall restrict myself to one significant fact; that he, ruler of all those lands, died leaving forty-seven Nasirite *drachmas* of silver in his treasury and a single piece of Tyrian gold whose weight I have forgotten. He used to give away whole provinces; when he conquered Amida [in Mesopotamia], Qara Arslan's son asked him for it and he gave it to him. I myself saw a whole series of deputations appear before him in Jerusalem when he had decided to leave for Damascus and there was no gold left in the treasury to give these people. I was so insistent on his giving them something that he sold a village belonging to the public revenue and distributed to them what he was given for it without seeing a single *drachma.* He was as generous when he was poor as he was when he was rich, and his treasurers kept certain reserves concealed from him for fear that some financial emergency might arise. For they knew that the moment

he heard of their existence he would spend them.

His Courage

The Prophet is reported to have said: "God loves courage, even in the killing of a serpent." Saladin was indeed one of the most courageous of men; brave, gallant, firm, intrepid in any circumstance. I remember when he was encamped facing a great Frankish army which was continuously growing with the addition of reinforcements and auxiliaries, and all the time his strength of will and tenacity of purpose increased. One evening more than seventy enemy ships arrived—I counted them myself—between the *asr* [first hour of the afternoon] prayer and sunset, and their only effect seemed to be to incense him the more. When winter came he had disbanded his army and faced the enemy with only a small detachment of troops....

Every day for as long as we were in close contact with the enemy he made it an inflexible rule to make one or two circuits of the enemy camp; in the thick of battle he would move through the ranks, accompanied only by a page with a war-horse led on a bridle. He would

traverse the whole army from the right wing to the left, creating a sense of unity and urging them to advance and to stand firm at the right time. He directed his troops from a commanding height and followed the enemy's movements from close at hand. He had certain sections of *hadith* read up and down the army's ranks. This arose from my observation that *hadith* had been read in every noble place, but one never heard of their being read before the ranks drawn up for battle, "and if Your Majesty were willing for this to be done it would be a fine thing." He authorized it, and a section of the *hadith* was taken down to the troops, together with one who had made a regular study of them, and the reading was held while we were all in the saddle, sometimes advancing and sometimes at a halt between the ranks of the two armies.

I never saw him find the enemy too numerous or too powerful. He would ponder and deliberate, exposing each aspect of the situation and taking the

necessary steps to deal with it, without becoming angry, for he was never irate. On the day of the great battle on the plain of Acre the center of the Muslim ranks was broken, drums and flags fell to the ground, but he stood firm with a handful of men until he was able to withdraw all his men to the hill and then lead them down into battle again, shaming them into turning and fighting, so that although there were almost 7000 infantry and cavalry killed that day God gave the Muslims victory over their enemies. He stood firm before overwhelming hordes of enemy soldiers until it became clear to him that the Muslims were exhausted, and then he agreed to a truce at the enemy's request. The Franks were also exhausted and had suffered even heavier losses than we, but they could expect reinforcements, as we could not, so that peace was in our interest, as emerged clearly from the developments that followed.

His Humanity

God has said: "and those among men who pardon others, and God loves those who act rightly [Koran 3, 128]." He was indulgent to those who failed and slow to wrath. I was on duty at his side at Marj Uyun before the Franks attacked Acre—may God make its reconquest easy!—It was his custom to ride on for as long as possible and then to dismount and have food served, which he would eat in company with his men before retiring to sleep in his private tent. When he awoke he would pray, and then withdraw, with me in attendance on him, to read a section of the *hadith* or Law: among other works that he read with me was an anthology of Sulaim ar-Razi, including the four sections of the

Law. One day he dismounted as usual and food was served. He was about to rise when he was told that it was almost the hour of prayer, so he sat down again and said: "Let us pray, and then let us go to bed." He sat and talked wearily. Everyone except his personal servants had withdrawn, when suddenly there appeared an ancient mameluk whom he held in high esteem, who presented him with a plea from someone fighting in the Holy War. "I am tired now," said the Sultan, "present it again a little later," but the man would not comply with this request. He held the plea up to the Sultan's august face, opening it so that he could read it. Saladin read the name written at the top, recognized it and said: "A worthy man." "Well then," said the other, "Your Majesty will inscribe your *placet*." "But there is no inkwell here," said the Sultan, for he was sitting at the opening of the tent, blocking the entrance, while the inkstand was at the back of the tent, which was a big one. But his interlocutor observed: "There is the inkstand, at the back of the tent!" which was nothing if not an invitation to Saladin to bring that very inkwell out. The Sultan turned, saw the inkstand and said: "By Allah, you are right!" He leaned on his left elbow, stretched out his right hand, took the inkstand, signed the plea.... Then I said: "God said to His prophet: 'You are truly a magnanimous man [Koran 58, 4],' and it seems to me that Your Majesty shares this quality with him," to which Saladin replied: "It did not cost anything; we heard what he wanted, and we wanted to recompense him." If a similar thing had happened to a private individual he would have lost his temper; and who would have been capable of replying to one of his subordinates in this way? This is the perfection of kindness and generosity, "and God will not let such goodness go unrewarded [Koran 9, 121]."

Sometimes, when the crowd thronged round him to present their pleas, the cushion on which he sat ended up crushed underfoot, yet he did not seem to mind at all. Once, while I was riding beside him, my mule took fright at the camels and kicked his thigh, injuring it; and he simply smiled. One rainy windy day as I was entering Jerusalem with him and the road was terribly muddy the mule splashed him and ruined all his clothes; but he smiled and refused to allow me to ride further back because of the incident.

Baha ad-Din
An-Nawadir as-Sultaniyya wa l-mahasin al-yusufiyya (*Sultanly Anecdotes and Josephly Virtues*), in *Arab Historians of the Crusades*, trans. from the Arabic by Francesco Gabrieli; trans. from the Italian by E. J. Costello, 1969

Opposite: Saladin entering the Holy City. Below: His tomb in Damascus.

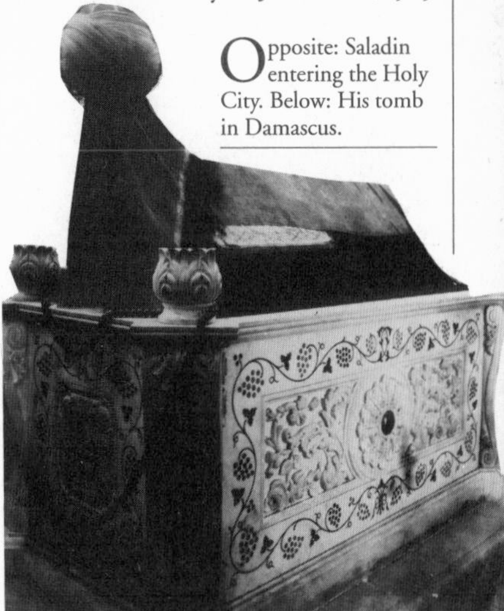

The Franks in Eastern Eyes

All the eastern peoples, Byzantine and Arab alike, agreed: the Franks were crude, brutal, and ignorant. Usama, emir of Shaizar, nonetheless also recognized in their knights the qualities of courage and sincerity, and in those who had lived in the East for a long time that of loyalty in their friendships.

The Franks in Byzantine Eyes

Anna Comnena, daughter of the Byzantine emperor, thought the crusaders were notable above all for their crudeness and brutality.

When all, including Godfrey, were assembled and after the oath had been sworn by every count, one nobleman dared to seat himself on the emperor's throne. Alexius endured this without a word, knowing of old the haughty temper of the Latins, but Count Baldwin went up to the old man, took him by the hand and made him rise. He gave him a severe reprimand: "You ought never to have done such a thing, especially after promising to be the emperor's liege-man. Roman emperors don't let their subject sit with them. That's the custom here and sworn liege-men of His Majesty should observe the customs of the country." The man said nothing to Baldwin, but

The Franks in eastern eyes: mighty beasts.

with a bitter glance at Alexius muttered some words to himself in his own language: "What a peasant! He sits alone while generals like these stand beside him!" Alexius saw his lips moving and calling one of the interpreters who understood the language asked him what he had said. Being told the words he made no comment to the man at the time, but kept the remark to himself. However, when they were all taking leave of him, he sent off the arrogant, impudent fellow and asked who he was, where he came from, and what his lineage was. "I am a pure Frank," he replied, "and of noble birth. One thing I know: at a cross-roads in the country where I was born is an ancient shrine; to this anyone who wishes to engage in single combat goes, prepared to fight; there he prays to God for help and there he stays awaiting the man who will dare to answer his challenge. At that cross-roads I myself have spent time, waiting and longing for the man who would fight—but there was never one who dared." Hearing this the emperor said, "If you didn't get your fight then, when you looked for it, now you have a fine opportunity for many. But I strongly recommend you not to take up position in the rear of the army, nor in the van; stand in the center with the [junior officers in the army]. I know the enemy's methods. I've had long experience of the Turk."

Anna Comnena
The Alexiad of Anna Comnena, Book X
trans. E. R. A. Sewter, 1969

The Franks in the Eyes of the Emir of Shaizar

Usama, emir of Shaizar, was also aware of the Franks' ignorance, but he made a distinction between the newcomers and the old-timers.

Godfrey of Bouillon, first ruler of the Latin kingdom of Jerusalem, was respected by the Muslims for his simplicity and piety.

A very important Frankish knight was staying in the camp of King Fulk, the son of Fulk. He had come on a pilgrimage and was going home again. We got to know one another, and became firm friends. He called me "brother" and an affectionate friendship grew up between us. When he was due to embark for the return journey he said to me, "I should be happy if you would send your son with me" (the boy, who was about fourteen years old, was beside me at the time), "so that he could meet the noblemen of the realm and learn the arts of politics and chivalry. On his return home he would be a truly cultivated man." A truly cultivated man would never be guilty of such a suggestion; my son might as well be taken prisoner as go off into the land of the Franks. I turned to my friend and said: "I assure you that I could desire nothing better for my son, but unfortunately the boy's grandmother, my mother, is very attached to him, and she would not even let him come away with me without extracting a promise from me that I would bring him back to her." "Your mother is still alive?" "Yes." "Then she must have her way."

The Oddness of Frankish Medicine

The ruler of Munaitira wrote to my uncle asking him to send a doctor to treat some of his followers who were ill. My uncle sent a Christian called Thabit. After only ten days he returned and we said "You cured them quickly!" This was his story: They took me to see a knight who had an abscess on his leg, and a woman with consumption. I applied a poultice to the leg, and the abscess opened and began to heal. I prescribed a cleansing and refreshing diet for the woman. Then there appeared a Frankish doctor, who said: "This man has no idea how to cure these people!" He turned to the knight and said: "Which would you prefer, to live with one leg or to die with two?" When the knight replied that he would rather live with one leg, he sent for a strong man and a sharp ax. They arrived and I stood by to watch. The doctor supported the leg on a block of wood, and said to the man: "Strike a mighty blow, and cut cleanly!" And there, before my eyes, the fellow struck the knight one blow, and then another, for the first had not finished the job. The marrow spurted out of the leg, and the patient died instantaneously. Then the doctor examined the woman and said: "She has a devil in her head who is in love with her. Cut her hair off!" This was done, and she went back to eating her usual Frankish food, garlic, and mustard, which made her illness worse. "The devil has got into her brain," pronounced the doctor. He took a razor and cut a cross on her head, and removed the brain so that the inside of the skull was laid bare. This he rubbed with salt; the woman died instantly. At this juncture I asked whether they had any further need of me, and as they had none I came away, having learnt things about medical methods that I never knew before.

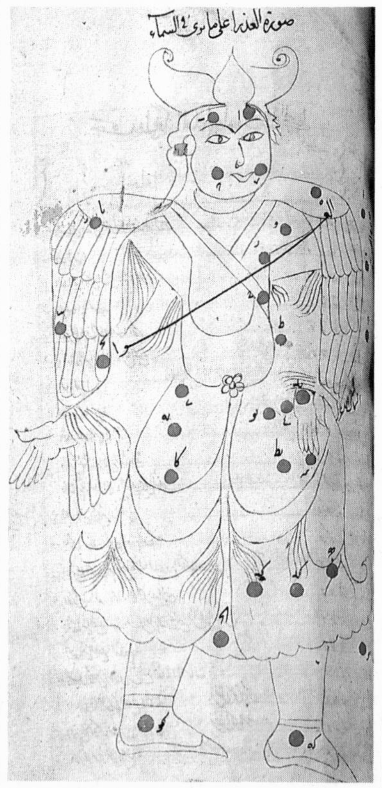

In the realm of science, Islam was far ahead of the West.

Orientalized Franks

There are some Franks who have settled in our land and taken to living like Muslims. These are better than those who have just arrived from their homelands, but they are the exception, and cannot be taken as typical. I came across one of them once when I sent a friend on business to Antioch, which was governed by [Theodore Sophianos], a friend of mine. One day he said to my friend: "A Frankish friend has invited me to visit him; come with me so that you can see how they live." "I went with him," said my friend, "and we came to the house of one of the old knights who came with the first expedition." This man had retired from the army, and was living on the income of the property he owned in Antioch. He had a fine table brought out, spread with a splendid selection of appetizing food. He saw that I was not eating, and said: "Don't worry, please; eat what you like, for I don't eat Frankish food. I have Egyptian cooks and eat only what they serve. No pig's flesh ever comes into my house!" So I ate, although cautiously, and then we left. Another day, as I was passing through the market, a Frankish woman advanced on me, addressing me in her barbaric language with words I found incomprehensible. A crowd of Franks gathered round us and I gave myself up for lost, when suddenly this knight appeared, saw me, and came up. "What do you want with this man?" "This man," she replied, "killed my brother Urso." This Urso was a knight from Apamea who was killed by a soldier from Hamat. The old man scolded the woman. "This man is a merchant, a city man, not a fighter, and he lives nowhere near where your brother was killed." Then he turned on the crowd, which melted away, and shook hands with me. Thus the fact that I ate at his table saved my life.

Usama ibn Munqidh
Kitab al-Itibar (*Book of Instruction with Illustrations*)
in *Arab Historians of the Crusades*
trans. from the Arabic
by Francesco Gabrieli
trans. from the Italian
by E. J. Costello
1969

The Frankish Fortresses

Of all the fortresses built by the Franks in Syria and Palestine, the most famous and the best-conserved is the Krak des Chevaliers in Syria. Ceded to the Hospitalers, it yielded before the onslaught of Baybars, despite its powerful defenses.

Plan of Margat Castle.

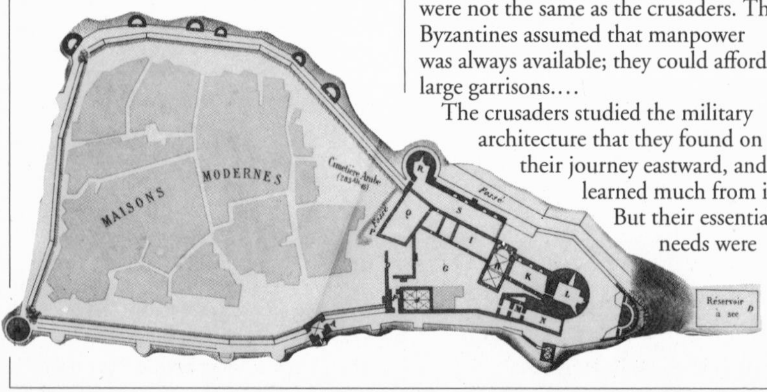

The Frankish Castles

The first buildings that the crusaders needed to construct were for their defense.... The first castle that can be dated with certainty is Count Raymond's at Mount Pilgrim, built in 1104 to provide him with headquarters while he besieged Tripoli. It was outside the town, though Muslim Tripoli was later built at its base.... But the first great age of castle-building began in the second decade of the 12th century, under Baldwin II, and was continued under Fulk, when such magnificent fortresses as Kerak of Moab, Beaufort and, further north, Sahyun, were constructed, as well as the smaller forts of Judaea, such as Blanchegarde and Ibelin.

The crusaders found military architecture far more highly developed in the East than in the West, where the stone-built castle was only now beginning to appear. The Romans had studied military defense as a science. The Byzantines, stimulated by the endless foreign invasions that they had to face, had evolved it to suit their needs, and the Arabs had learned from them. But the Byzantines' problems were not the same as the crusaders. The Byzantines assumed that manpower was always available; they could afford large garrisons....

The crusaders studied the military architecture that they found on their journey eastward, and learned much from it. But their essential needs were

Fortress of Sidon.

different. They were always short of manpower and could not maintain large garrisons. Their castles therefore had to be far stronger and easier to defend. The site must be chosen for its defensive qualities. Every slope and hillock must be used to the fullest advantage, and, as scouts to carry messages could seldom be spared, each stronghold should be able to see and signal to its neighbor. Walls had to be far thicker and taller, to be able to stand up to a direct attack; for the defense of outworks involved too many men. At the same time the castle must serve as a residence for the lord and an office for his administration. The Franks brought their feudal methods with them and they were governing an alien people. The castle was the seat of local government. Its enceinte [enclosing wall] should also be large enough to give protection to flocks and herds during the frequent enemy raids. The castle, in fact, played a far more important part among the Franks than ever among the Byzantines or the Arabs.

In the West the castle was as yet no more than the solid square keep or *donjon*, of a type perfected by the Normans. It was inadequate for the requirements of Outremer [overseas]. The crusaders were obliged to be pioneers. They borrowed many ideas from the Byzantines. It was from them that they learned the use of machicolation [openings for discharging weapons], and the value of placing towers along the curtain wall; though there they soon made an amendment, as they discovered that a rounded tower gave a wider range than the rectangular towers that the Byzantines preferred. Their smaller castles built in the earlier 12th century, such as Belvoir, were built on the usual

Byzantine design, with a more or less rectangular outer wall, studded with towers, enclosing a central space which contained the keep. But the sites were chosen so as to dispense with elaborate outworks, and the whole construction was far more solid. Byzantine work was often incorporated. At Sahyun the wide Byzantine fosses [moats] were completed by a narrow channel, ninety feet deep, cut through the solid rock. The Franks also added the portcullis, which had not been used in the East since Roman times, and the bent entrance....

The larger castles were naturally more complicated. A fortress such as Kerak had to house not only the lord and his family but also the soldiers and clerks required for their administration of a province.... The plan varied according to the terrain of the assiette, the area on which the castle was situated. The keep was still a simple rectangular tower, on the Norman model, usually with only one entrance. The masonry was solid and plain, but some attempt was made to decorate the residential quarters and the chapel....

As the 12th century advanced, there were certain changes in the plan of castles. It came to be considered more logical to put the keep, which was the strongest portion of the castle, at the weakest section of the enceinte; and the keep itself was usually rounded rather than rectangular, as a rounded surface resisted bombardment more effectively. More doors and posterns were provided. The size of castles tended to increase, particularly when the military orders built castles for themselves or took over castles from the lay nobility.... The larger fortresses, such as Krak [des Chevaliers] or Athlit, were military towns capable of housing several thousand fighting men and the servants necessary for such a community. But they were seldom filled to capacity. The defenses were now usually strengthened by the use of the double, concentric enceinte. The great Hospitaler castles, such as Krak and Margat, had a double girdle. The Templars followed the same system at Safita, but as a rule they

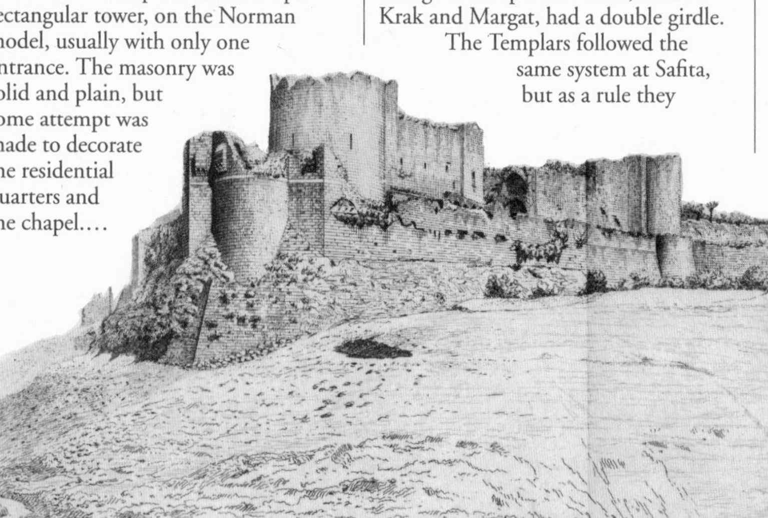

preferred the single enceinte; their chief 13th-century castles, Tortosa and Athlit, kept to the earlier pattern, but in both cases the longer sections of the walls rose straight from the sea. Across the peninsula which joined Athlit to the land there was a complicated double line....

Other 13th-century improvements were the carefully smooth facing of the curtain walls, to give less hold to grappling-ladders, the wider use of machicolation, and of loopholes for archers, which were now usually given a downward slant and sometimes a stirrup-shaped base, and greater complication in the entrance gates. At Krak there was a long covered approach, commanded by loopholes in the side-walls, then three right-angled corners, a portcullis, and four separate gates. Posterns were provided at unexpected corners, a device first introduced by the Byzantines.

These huge fortresses, with their solid masonry, superbly situated on crags and mountain-tops, seemed impregnable in the days before gunpowder was known. The terrain usually made the use of ladders impracticable, nor could siege-towers to dominate the walls be brought up unless there was some flat ground outside and no fosse. It was often hard enough for besiegers to find a close enough site on which to place mangonels or balistas for hurling rocks. The chief technical danger was the mine. Engineers would dig a tunnel under the walls, propping it up as they went with wooden posts, which were eventually set alight with brushwood, causing the tunnel-chamber, and with it the masonry above to collapse. But mining was impossible if the castle was built, like Krak, on solid rock. When a castle fell it was usually for other reasons. In spite of store-rooms and cisterns, famine and thirst were real dangers. The lack of manpower often meant that the defenses could not be properly maintained. The kingdom often could not afford to send a relieving force, and that knowledge induced pessimism among the garrison.

Steven Runciman
A History of the Crusades, vol. 3
1954

The Stages in the Construction of Krak des Chevaliers

When did the first Frankish wave of construction occur? The outpost occupied by the Kurdish military and established by the Muslim sultans at Hisn al-Akrad, "the castle of the Kurds," a term that Arab history writers continued to use throughout the Middle Ages to designate Krak, was intended only as a small fortress of little significance, and no trace of it has ever been found....

At least for a while, the crusaders had to make do with the fortifications they

Margat Castle, seen from the southeast.

captured, such as the castle of the Kurds and the Byzantine fortress that remains in the compound of Sahyun Castle, places the crusaders occupied from the early years of the 12th century.

Therefore, it is necessary to begin with the time when Krak was occupied by the Hospitalers, in 1142, to find the oldest parts of the castle still visible today. Even so, the earliest construction carried out by the Franks could not have lasted to the present, for in 1157 and 1170, earthquakes caused considerable damage to the Frankish fortresses in Syria. An Arab chronicler emphasized the extent of the damage sustained by Krak in 1170, where, it was said, not a single wall remained standing. He added that the violent tremor occurred on a festival, and that the Christians watched in horror as the vaults of their churches collapsed. As the author had just been writing about Krak, it seems reasonable to conclude that the castle's church was among those destroyed. The church at Krak today is the oldest part of the remaining fortress. It would have been built after 1170, presumably soon after the incident, as the Hospitalers, being a religious as well as military order, could not do without a church....

Above and opposite: Sahyun Castle.

We have come to the conclusion that the oldest elements that have survived to the present date after 1170. They are characterized by rusticated masonry. The remains are more extensive than one might have supposed, and almost the entire enclosing wall, hidden by additions made in the course of the second period of construction, except in the area of the chapel, has been preserved.

The second period of construction is represented by the three big towers at the south end, by the large embankments into which they are set, the embankment of the western aspect, and by the work on the enclosing wall.

We believe that these various constructions, composed of a large and a medium arrangement of smooth stones, date from the first years of the 13th century. New earthquakes, in 1201 and 1202, must have caused some damage to the fortress and led the architects to conceive those great

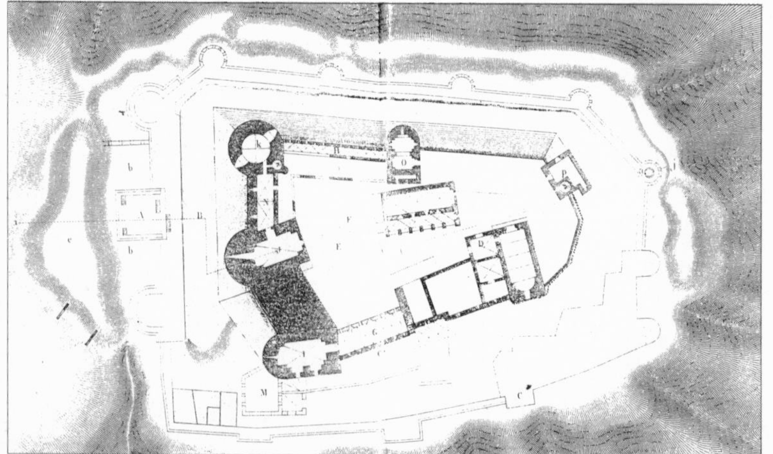

Restored view and plan of Krak des Chevaliers.

embankments, which, as we have said, must have reinforced the walls.

Paul Deschamps
Le Krak des Chevaliers, 1934

The Capture of Krak des Chevaliers

Hisn al-Akrad was not among the cities taken by Saladin but remained in Frankish hands until al-Malik az-Zahir Rukn ad-Din Baibars led the 669 [1271] expedition against Tripoli of which we have already spoken. He besieged Hisn al-Akrad on 9 rajab [21 February]; on 20 rajan [4 March] the suburbs were taken and al-Malik al-Mansur, ruler of Hamat, arrived with his army. The Sultan went on to meet him, descended from his horse when al-Mansur did and advanced beneath his banners without bodyguards or equerries as a gesture of courtesy to the Lord of Hamat. At his command a tent was brought and pitched for him. The amir of Sahyun, saif ad-Din, and Najm ad-Din, the Grand Master of the Ismailites also arrived.

At the end of rajab work was completed on a large number of catapults. On 7 shaban [22 March] the bastions were taken by storm and an emplacement was built from which the sultan could draw a bow at the enemy. Then Baybars began to distribute gifts of money and robes of honor.

On 16 shaban [31 March] a breach was made in one of the towers of the fortress, our soldiers went up to attack, got up into the fort and took possession of it, while the Franks withdrew to the keep. A whole group of Franks and Christians was then set free by the sultan as a pious offering in the name of al-Malik as-Said [son of Baybars]. The catapults were then moved into the fortress and directed on the keep. At this point the Sultan wrote certain letters as if they had been written by the Frankish general in Tripoli, ordering them to surrender. They begged that their lives should be spared, which was granted on condition that they returned to their homelands. On Tuesday 24 shaban [7 April] the Franks left the fort and were sent home.

Ibn al-Furat
Tarikh ad-duwal wa l-muluk (*The History of the Dynasties and the Kings*), in *Arab Historians of the Crusades,* trans. from the Arabic by Francesco Gabrieli; trans. from the Italian by E. J. Costello
1969

Northwest tower of Krak des Chevaliers.

Lawrence of Arabia

Lawrence of Arabia (T. E. Lawrence) published two volumes on Frankish fortresses in Syria and Palestine, Crusader Castles, *1936, from which these sketches and this photograph are taken.*

Krak des Chevaliers (below left and above) and Pilgrim Castle (below).

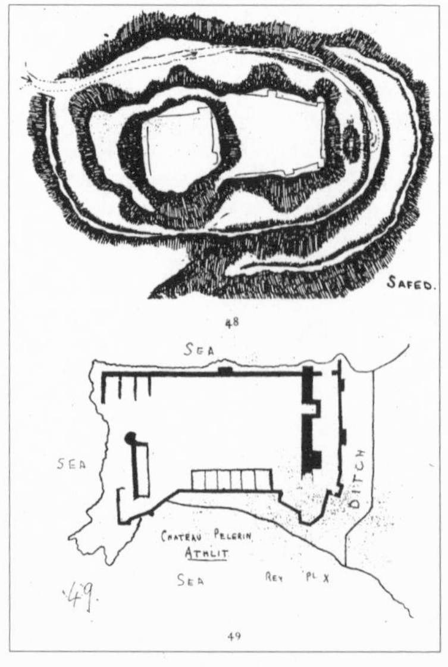

SAHYUN. The South-East Corner.

Pencil and ink drawings of Sahyun Castle.

The Crusades: A Summing Up

After a long period during which the crusades were viewed as a positive event for Christianity, historians of both the western and eastern worlds have arrived at much more circumspect conclusions.

Coin from the kingdom of Jerusalem.

The Crusades: A Vast Fiasco

The crusades were launched to save Eastern Christendom from the Muslims. When they ended the whole of Eastern Christendom was under Muslim rule. When Pope Urban preached his great sermon at Clermont the Turks seemed about to threaten the Bosporus. When Pope Pius II preached the last crusade the Turks were crossing the Danube....

Seen in the perspective of history the whole crusading movement was a vast fiasco.... There was not a country that failed to send soldiers to fight for Christendom in the East. Jerusalem was in the mind of every man and woman. Yet the efforts to hold or recapture the Holy City were peculiarly capricious and inept. Nor did these efforts have the effect on the general history of western Europeans that might have been expected from them. The era of the crusades is one of the most important in the history of western civilization. When it began, western Europe was only just emerging from the long period of barbarian invasions that we call the Dark Ages. When it ended, the great burgeoning that we call the Renaissance had just begun. But we cannot assign any direct part in this development to the crusaders themselves. The crusaders had nothing to do with the new security in the West, which enabled merchants and scholars to travel as they pleased. There was already access to the stored-up learning of the Muslim world through Spain.... Throughout the crusading period itself, it was Sicily rather than the lands of Outremer that provided a meeting place for Arab, Greek, and western culture. Intellectually, Outremer added next to nothing....

It was only in some aspects of the political development of western Europe that the crusades left a mark. One of Pope Urban's expressed aims in preaching the crusades was to find some useful work for the turbulent and bellicose barons who otherwise spent their energy on civil wars at home; and the removal of large sections of that unruly element to the East undoubtedly helped the rise of monarchical power in the West, to the ultimate detriment of the papacy. But meanwhile the papacy itself benefited. The pope had launched the crusade as an international Christian movement under his leadership; and its initial success greatly enhanced his power and prestige....

Apart from the widening of the spiritual dominion of Rome, the chief benefit obtained by Western Christendom from the crusades was negative. When they began the main seats of civilization were in the East, at Constantinople and at Cairo. When they ended, civilization had moved its headquarters to Italy and the young countries of the West. The crusades were not the only cause for the decline of the Muslim world. The invasions of the Turks had already undermined the Abbasid caliphate of Baghdad and even without the crusade they might have ultimately brought down the Fatimid caliphate of Egypt. But had it not been for the incessant irritation of the wars against the Franks, the Turks might well have been integrated into the Arab world and provided for it a new vitality and strength without destroying its basic unity....

But the real harm done to Islam by the crusades was subtler. The Islamic State was a theocracy whose political welfare depended on the caliphate, the line of priest-kings to whom custom had given a hereditary succession. The crusading attack came when the Abbasid caliphate was unable politically or geographically to lead Islam against it; and the Fatimid caliphs, as heretics, could not command a wide enough allegiance. The leaders who arose to defeat the Christians, men like Nureddin and Saladin, were heroic figures who were given respect and devotion, but they were adventurers. The Ayyubids, for all their ability, could never be accepted as the supreme rulers of Islam, because they were not caliphs; they were not even descended from the Prophet. They had no proper place in the theocracy of Islam.

Christianity allowed from the outset a distinction between the things that are Caesar's and the things that are God's and so, when the medieval conception of the undivided political City of God broke down, its vitality was unimpaired. But Islam was conceived as a political and religious unity. This unity had been cracked before the crusades; but the events of those centuries made the cracks too wide to be mended. The great Ottoman sultans achieved a superficial repair, but only for a time. The cracks have endured to this day.

Even more harmful was the effect of the Holy War on the spirit of Islam. Any religion that is based on an exclusive Revelation is bound to show some contempt for the unbeliever. But Islam was not intolerant in its early days. Muhammad himself considered that Jews and Christians had received a partial Revelation and were therefore not to be persecuted. Under the early caliphs the Christians played an honorable part in Arab society. A remarkably large number of the early Arabic thinkers and writers were Christians, who provided a useful intellectual stimulus; for the Muslims, with their reliance on the Word of God, given once and for all time in the Koran, tended to remain static and unenterprising in their thought. Nor was the rivalry of the caliphate with Christian Byzantium entirely unfriendly. Scholars and technicians passed to and fro between the two empires to their mutual benefit. The holy war begun by the Franks ruined these good relations. The savage intolerance shown by the crusaders was answered by growing intolerance among the Muslims. The broad humanity of Saladin and his family was soon to be rare among their fellow-believers. By the time of the Mamluks, the Muslims were as narrow as the Franks....

The harm done by the crusades to Islam was small in comparison with that done by them to Eastern Christendom. Pope Urban II had bidden the crusaders go forth that the Christians of the East might be helped and rescued. It was a strange rescue; for when the work was over, Eastern Christendom lay under infidel domination and the crusaders themselves had done all they could to prevent its recovery. When they set themselves up in the East they treated their Christian subjects no better than the caliph had done before them. Indeed, they were sterner, for they interfered in the religious practices of the local churches....

The real disaster of the crusades was the inability of Western Christendom to comprehend Byzantium. Throughout the ages there have always been hopeful politicians who believe that if

Pope Alexander III flanked by Frederick Barbarossa and his wife.

only the peoples of the world could come together they would love and understand each other. It is a tragic delusion. So long as Byzantium and the West had little to do with each other their relations were friendly. Western pilgrims and soldiers of fortune were welcomed in the imperial city and went home to tell of its splendors; but there were not enough of them to make friction.... But with the Norman determination to expand into the eastern Mediterranean a new disquieting era began. Byzantine interests were flung into sharp conflict with those of a western people....

The determination of the westerners to conquer and colonize the lands of Byzantium was disastrous for the interests of Outremer. It was more disastrous still for European civilization. Constantinople was still the center of the civilized Christian world. In the pages of Villehardouin we see reflected the impression that it made on the knights that had come from France and Italy to conquer it. They could not believe that so superb a city could exist on earth; it was of all cities the sovereign. Like most barbarian invaders, the men of the Fourth Crusade did not intend to destroy what they found. They meant to share it and dominate it. But their greed and their clumsiness led them to indulge in irreparable destruction....

To the crusaders themselves their failures were inexplicable. They were fighting for the cause of the Almighty; and if faith and logic were correct, that cause should have triumphed. In the first flush of success they entitled their chronicles the *Gesta Dei per Francos*, God's work done by the hands of the Franks. But after the First Crusade there followed a long train of disasters; and even the victories of the Third Crusade were incomplete and unsure. There were evil forces about which thwarted God's work. At first the blame could be laid on Byzantium, on the schismatic emperor and his ungodly people who refused to recognize the divine mission of the crusaders. But after the Fourth Crusade that excuse could no longer be maintained; yet things went steadily worse. Moralist preachers might claim that God was angry with His warriors because of their sins.... In fact it was not so much wickedness as stupidity that ruined the holy wars. Yet such is human nature that a man will admit far more readily to being a sinner than a fool. No one among the crusaders would admit that their real crimes were a willful and narrow ignorance and an irresponsible lack of foresight....

The triumphs of the crusade were the triumphs of faith. But faith without wisdom is a dangerous thing. By the inexorable laws of history the whole world pays for the crimes and follies of each of its citizens. In the long sequence of interaction and fusion between Orient and Occident out of which our civilization has grown, the crusades were a tragic and destructive episode. The historian as he gazes back across the centuries at their gallant story must find his admiration overcast by sorrow at the witness that it bears to the limitations of human nature. There was so much courage and so little honor, so much devotion and so little understanding. High ideals were besmirched by cruelty and greed, enterprise and endurance by a blind and narrow self-righteousness; and the holy war itself was nothing more than a long act of intolerance in the name of God, which is the sin against the Holy Ghost.

Steven Runciman
A History of the Crusades, vol. 3, 1954

The Heavy Liabilities of the Crusades

To the knights and peasants of the 11th century the crusade probably seemed to be an outlet for the excess population of the West, even if this impulse was neither clearly formulated nor felt by the crusaders. Furthermore, the desire for lands, wealth, and knights' fees overseas was a major attraction. However, the crusades, even before they came to an end in complete failure, did not satisfy the westerners' hunger for land. They soon had to look for the solution, which the Outremer had failed to give them, in Europe, chiefly in the expansion of agriculture.... The crusades brought western Europe neither commercial growth, which had arisen out of earlier links with the Muslim world and out of the internal development of the western economy, nor skills and products, which came by other routes; nor intellectual equipment, which was provided by translation centers and libraries in Greece, Italy (above all in Sicily), and Spain, where contacts were close and productive, quite unlike Palestine. The crusades did not even bring a taste for luxury and soft habits, thought by gloomy western moralists to be a prerogative of the East, the poisoned gift of the infidels to the ingenuous crusaders who were defenseless before eastern charms and charmers.... On the contrary, they helped to impoverish the West, especially the knight class. Far from creating a unity of mind throughout Western Christianity they actually encouraged awakening national hostilities to become poisoned.... Furthermore, the crusades built a decisive barrier between the westerners and the Byzantines. Hostility between Latins and Greeks grew sharper from crusade to crusade, and culminated in the Fourth Crusade and the sack of Constantinople by the crusaders in 1204. Far from softening manners, the fanaticism of holy war led the crusaders on the worst excesses, from the pogroms perpetuated on their journeys to the massacres and sackings such as those of Jerusalem in 1099 and Constantinople in 1204, which we can read about not only in the accounts of Muslim or Byzantine chroniclers but also in the accounts of Latin chroniclers. Financing the crusades was a motive or a pretext for heavier papal taxation and for the ill-conceived practice of selling indulgences. Finally, the military orders, which were powerless to defend and guard the Holy Land, fell back on the West, where they took to all sorts of financial and military exactions. This was the debit side of the expeditions. Probably the apricot was the only benefit brought back from the crusades by the Christians.

Jacques Le Goff
Medieval Civilization, 1988

The Middle East Again in Collision

Although the epoch of the crusades ignited a genuine economic and cultural revolution in western Europe, in the Orient these holy wars led to long centuries of decadence and obscurantism. Assaulted from all quarters, the Muslim world turned in on itself.... Henceforth progress was the embodiment of "the other." Modernism became alien. Should cultural and religious identity be affirmed by rejecting this modernism, which the West symbolized? Or, on the contrary, should the road of modernization be embarked upon with resolution, thus risking loss of identity? Neither Iran, nor Turkey, nor the Arab world has ever succeeded in resolving this dilemma. Even today we can observe a lurching alternation between phases of forced westernization and phases of extremist, strongly xenophobic traditionalism.

The Arab world—simultaneously fascinated and terrified by these Franj [Franks], whom they encountered as barbarians and defeated, but who subsequently managed to dominate the earth—cannot bring itself to consider the crusades a mere episode in the bygone past. It is often surprising to discover the extent to which the attitude of the Arabs (and of Muslims in general) towards the West is still influenced, even today, by events that supposedly ended some seven centuries ago.

Today, on the eve of the third millennium, the political and religious

Political propaganda: Saddam Hussein of Iraq places himself beside Saladin. Overleaf: Monuments of Frankish Syria.

leaders of the Arab world constantly refer to Saladin, to the fall of Jerusalem and its recapture. In the popular mind, and in some official discourse too, Israel is regarded as a new crusader state. Of the three divisions of the Palestine Liberation Army, one bears the name Hattin and the other Ayn Jalut [sights of two Muslim victories]. In his days of glory, President Nasser [of Egypt] was regularly compared to Saladin, who, like him, had united Syria and Egypt—and even Yemen! The Arabs perceived the Suez expedition of 1956 as a crusade by the French and the English, similar to that of 1191.

It is true that there are disturbing resemblances. It is difficult not to think of President Sadat when we hear Sibt Idn al-Jawzi speaking to the people of Damascus and denouncing the "betrayal" of al-Kamil, the ruler of Cairo, who dared to acknowledge sovereignty over the Holy City. It is tempting to confound past and present when we read of a struggle between Damascus and Jerusalem for control of Golan Heights or the Bekaa Valley. It is hard not to daydream when we read Usamah's reflections about the military superiority of the invaders.

In a Muslim world under constant attack, it is impossible to prevent the emergence of a sense of persecution, which among certain fanatics takes the form of a dangerous obsession. The Turk Mehmet Ali Agca, who tried to shoot the pope on 13 May 1981, had expressed himself in a letter in these terms: "I have decided to kill John Paul II, supreme commander of the Crusades." Beyond this individual act, it seems clear that the Arab East still sees the West as a natural enemy. Against that enemy, any hostile action—be it political, military, or based on oil—is considered no more than legitimate vengeance. And there can be no doubt that the schism between these two worlds dates from the crusades, deeply felt by the Arabs, even today, as an act of rape.

Amin Maalouf
The Crusades through Arab Eyes
trans. Jon Rothschild, 1985

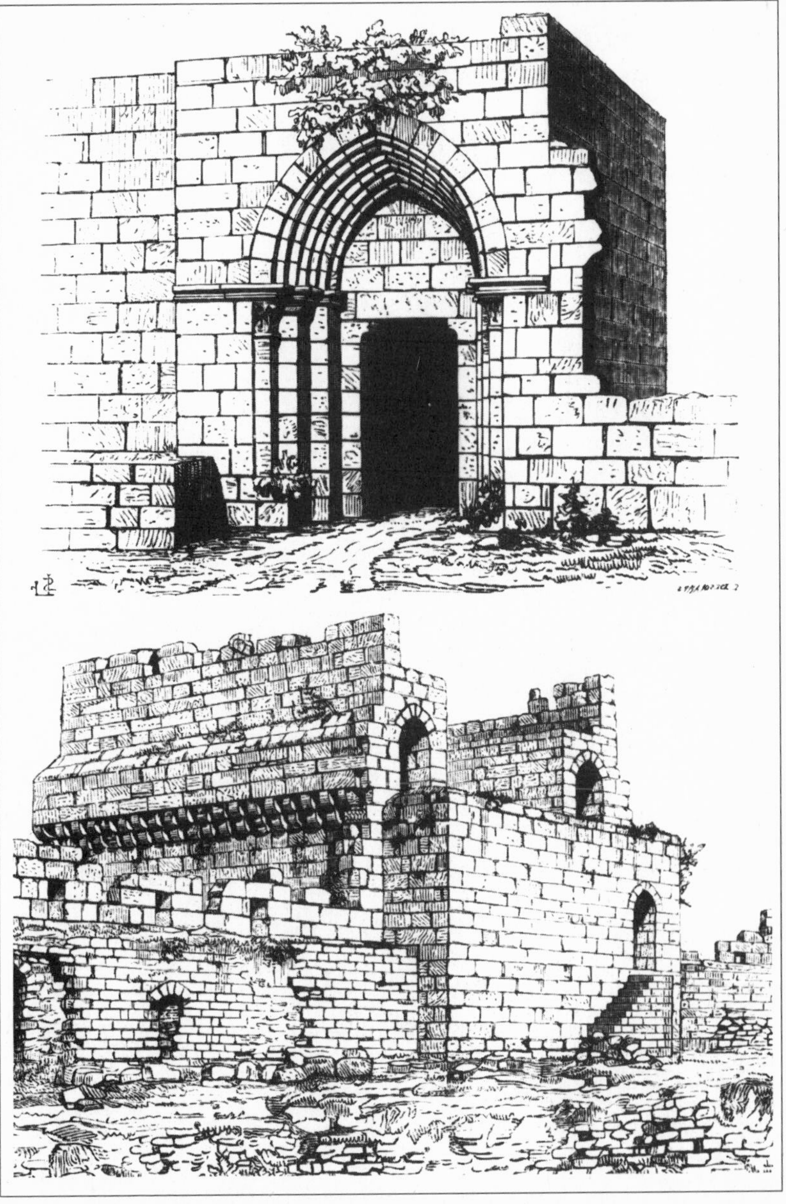

Chronology
The Crusades in the East

THE ARABS BEFORE THE CRUSADES

622: Muhammad's emigration (the Hegira) to Medina; beginning of Muslim calendar.
633: Arab conquest of Persia.
637: Arab conquest of Palestine and Syria.
687: Construction of Dome of the Rock (mosque of Umar) begins in Jerusalem.
711–7: Arab conquest of Spain.
732: Saracen Muslims repelled from France in battle of Poitiers.
842–902: Conquest of Sicily by Arabs.
1055: Seljuk Turks seize Baghdad.
1071: Seljuks crush Byzantines at battle of Manzikert and seize Asia Minor.

THE FIRST CRUSADE (1096–9)

1095: Byzantine Emperor Alexius Comnenus appeals to West for help against the Turks; Pope Urban II calls for Christians to rescue the Holy Land at Council of Clermont, France.
1096: Peter the Hermit heads People's Crusade, which leads to massacre of Jews in the Rhineland; Kilij Arslan crushes crusade.
1097: First great crusading expedition reaches Asia Minor; crusaders first victories at Nicaea and Dorylaeum.
1098: Crusaders take Edessa and Antioch, founding first two crusader states in the East.
1099: In July crusaders capture Jerusalem, and found Frankish kingdom of Jerusalem, with Godfrey of Bouillon as ruler.
1100: Venice and kingdom of Jerusalem make a trade pact.
1100–18: Reign of Baldwin I, king of Jerusalem.
1101: Second wave of crusaders is defeated in Asia Minor.
1104: Crusaders capture Acre; Muslim victory at Harran; Byzantines reclaim Antioch from Franks.
1108: Bohemond submits to sovereignty of Alexius I.
1109: Capture of Tripoli and creation of last Latin state.
1110: Baldwin I captures Sidon and Beirut
1113: Turks advance; Baldwin I is defeated at Tiberias.
1114: Crusaders make an alliance with *atabeg* of Damascus.
1115: Franks, allied with Aleppo and Damascus, defeat Mosul ruler at battle of Tel-Danith.
1118: Baldwin I invades Egypt.
1118–31: Reign of Baldwin II of Jerusalem.
1119: Crusader defeat at "Field of Blood"; Roger of Salerno is killed.
1124: Crusaders capture Tyre.
1128: Zengi becomes ruler of Aleppo and Mosul.
1130: Zengi takes Hama and attacks Antioch.
1131–43: Reign of Fulk I of Jerusalem.
1137: Fulk surrenders to Zengi at Montferrand.
1138: John II Comnenus forces Raymond, prince of Antioch, to recognize his sovereignty
1139: Jerusalem and Damascus unite against Zengi.
1140: Zengi lifts siege of Damascus.
1144: Zengi takes Edessa; crusaders lose first of their states.

THE SECOND CRUSADE (1147–9)

1146: Zengi is murdered; succeeded by his son, Nureddin; Saint Bernard preaches Second Crusade at Vézelay. It was led by Louis VII of France and Conrad III of Germany.
1148: Siege of Damascus fails; Conrad returns to Europe (followed by Louis the next year).
1149: Consecration of church of the Holy Sepulcher in Jerusalem; Nureddin defeats Raymond of Poitiers, prince of Antioch.
1153: Baldwin III captures Ashkelon from Fatimids.
1154: Nureddin takes Damascus.
1156: Reginald of Châtillon sacks Byzantine island of Cyprus.
1158: Baldwin III marries niece of Emperor Manuel I.
1159: Antioch submits to sovereignty of Byzantine emperor.
1160: Nureddin captures Reginald of Châtillon.
1163: Amalric I succeeds Baldwin III.
1163–9: Amalric leads expeditions to Egypt.
1164: Nureddin's lieutenant Shirkuh enters Egypt; Amalric I and Egyptian ruler Shawar ally against Shirkuh; Egypt becomes Frankish "protectorate."
1169: Amalric fails in Egypt; Shirkuh captures Cairo; Saladin becomes vizier in Egypt; Franks and Byzantines form an alliance; Frankish-Byzantine siege of Damietta fails.
1171: Saladin ends Fatimid caliphate of Cairo and proclaims Abbasid caliphate.
1174: Nureddin and Amalric I die; accession of Baldwin IV, "Leper King"; Saladin takes power in Syria.
1176: Seljuks defeat Byzantines at Myriocephalum.
1177: Baldwin IV defeats Saladin at Montgisard.
1183: Saladin captures Aleppo.
1185: Saladin makes four-year truce with Franks; Baldwin V accedes to throne, but is soon succeeded by Guy of Lusignan.
1187: Reginald of Châtillon breaks treaty and ambushes Muslim caravan; Saladin retaliates, crushing crusaders at Hattin and reconquering Jerusalem.

THE THIRD CRUSADE (1189–92)

1187: Pope Gregory VIII proclaims Third Crusade, led by Frederick I (Barbarossa), Philip I (Philip Augustus), and Richard I (Lion-Heart).
1188: Saladin controls all Frankish territory except Tripoli, Tyre, and Antioch.
1189: Guy of Lusignan sets siege to Acre.
1190: Frederick Barbarossa arrives in Asia Minor, captures Iconium, and then drowns.
1191: Crusade of Philip Augustus and Richard the Lion-Heart; Richard invades Cyprus and captures Acre; Saladin is defeated at Arsuf.
1192: Guy of Lusignan buys Cyprus from Richard; Henry of Champagne is named king of Jerusalem; Richard and Saladin declare truce at Jaffa; Richard fails to take Jerusalem and returns to West (where he becomes a prisoner in Austria).
1193: Saladin dies.
1197: Henry of Champagne dies; Beirut recaptured; John I of Ibelin becomes its lord.

THE FOURTH CRUSADE (1202–4)

1199: Pope Innocent III calls for a crusade.
1204: Crusaders sack Constantinople and found Eastern Latin Empire (1204–61).

THE FIFTH CRUSADE (1217–21)

1218–9: Crusaders invade Egypt and take Damietta.
1221: Expedition to Cairo ends in disaster; Damietta falls.

THE SIXTH CRUSADE (1228–9)

1229: Treaty of Jaffa with sultan of Egypt, delivers Jerusalem to Frederick II for ten years.
1239: Setback of Sixth Crusade; appeal made for another crusade.
1244: Christians are defeated at Gaza; Khwarezm Turks definitively take back Jerusalem.

THE SEVENTH CRUSADE OR THE FIRST CRUSADE OF (SAINT) LOUIS IX (1248–50)

1248: Saint Louis lands at Cyprus.
1249: Saint Louis captures Damietta.
1250: Battle of Al-Mansura and Saint Louis's surrender; he abandons Damietta in exchange for his freedom; Mamluks take power in Egypt.
1250–4: Saint Louis reorganizes Palestine and Syria.
1258: Mongols sack Baghdad and kill last Abbasid caliph.
1260: Mamluks defeat Mongols at Ayn Jalut.
1260–77: Reign of Baybars, sultan of Mamluks.
1261: Greeks reoccupy Constantinople.
1265: Baybars captures Caesarea and Arsuf.
1268: Baybars captures Jaffa and Antioch.

THE EIGHTH CRUSADE OR THE SECOND CRUSADE OF LOUIS IX (1270)

1270: Saint Louis dies in Tunisia.
1274–5: Mamluks lay waste Cilicia.
1277: Charles of Anjou claims kingdom of Jerusalem and captures Acre.
1282: Henry II of Lusignan, king of Cyprus, becomes king of Jerusalem.
1289: Mamluks take Tripoli.
1291: Mamluks take Acre, destroying last holdout of crusader states.

Adapted from Francesco Gabrieli, *Arab Historians of the Crusades,* London, Routledge & Kegan Paul, 1969.

Further Reading

The Alexiad of Anna Comnena, trans. E. R. A. Sewter, Harmondsworth, Penguin Books, 1969

Billings, Malcolm, *The Cross and the Crescent: a History of the Crusades*, New York, Sterling, and London, BBC, 1987

Bridge, Antony, *The Crusades*, New York and London, Granada, 1980

Brundage, James A., *Crusades: A Documentary Survey*, Milwaukee, Marquette University Press, 1962

Elisséeff, Nikita, *Nur ad-Din: Un Grand Prince Musulman de Syrie au Temps des Croisades, 511–569*, Damascus, 1967, 3 vols.

Fulcher of Chartres, *A History of the Expedition to Jerusalem: 1095–1127*, trans. Frances Rita Ryan, Knoxville, University of Tennessee Press, 1969

Gabrieli, Francesco, ed., *Arab Historians of the Crusades*, London, Routledge & Kegan Paul, 1969

Glubb, John Bagot, *A Short History of the Arab Peoples*, New York, Stein and Day, and London, Hodder and Stoughton, 1969

Grousset, René, *The Epic of the Crusades,* New York, Orion Press, 1970

Hitti, Philip K., *History of the Arabs*, New York, St. Martin's Press, and London, Macmillan & Co., 1937

Hourani, Albert, *A History of the Arab Peoples*, Cambridge, Mass., Harvard University Press, and London, Faber and Faber, 1991

Joinville, Jean de, and G. de Villehardouin, *Chronicles of the Crusades*, trans. M. R. B. Shaw, Harmondsworth, Penguin Books, 1969

Le Goff, Jacques, *Medieval Civilization, 400–1500*, trans. Julia Barrow, Oxford, Basil Blackwell, 1988

Maalouf, Amin, *The Crusades through Arab Eyes*, trans. Jon Rothschild, London, Al Saqi, 1984, and New York, Schocken Books, 1985

Mayer, Hans Eberhard, *The Crusades*, trans. John Gillingham, Oxford University Press, 1972

Morrisson, Cecile, *Les Croisades,* Paris, PUF, 4th ed., 1984

Oldenbourg, Zoë, *The Crusades*, trans. Anne Carter, New York, Random House, and London, Weidenfeld and Nicolson, 1966

Prawer, Joshua, *The World of the Crusaders*, London, Weidenfeld and Nicolson, 1972

———, *Crusader Institutions*, Oxford, Clarendon Press, 1980

———, *The Latin Kingdom of Jerusalem*, London, Weidenfeld and Nicolson, 1972

Richard, Jean, *Saint Louis: Crusader King of France*, ed. S. D. Lloyd, trans. J. Birrell, Cambridge University Press, 1992

———, *The Latin Kingdom of Jerusalem*, trans. Janet Shirley, Oxford, North Holland Publishing Co., 1979, 2 vols.

Riley-Smith, Jonathan, *The Crusades: A Short History*, New Haven, Yale University Press, and London, Athlone, 1987

———, ed., *The Oxford Illustrated History of the Crusades*, Oxford University Press, 1995

Runciman, Steven, *A History of the Crusades*, Cambridge University Press, 1951–4, rev. ed., 1980, 3 vols.

Setton, Kenneth M., *A History of the Crusades*, Madison, University of Wisconsin Press, 2nd ed., 1969–89, 6 vols.

———, *The Papacy and the Levant (1204–1571)*, Philadelphia, American Philosophical Society, 1976, 4 vols.

Siberry, Elizabeth, *Criticism of Crusading, 1095–1274*, Oxford University Press, 1985

Smail, Raymond Charles, *Crusading Warfare (1097–1193)*, Cambridge University Press, 1956

———, *The Crusaders in Syria and the Holy Land*, London, Thames and Hudson, 1973

Usamah ibn Munqidh, *Memoirs of an Arab-Syrian Gentleman and Warrior in the Period of the Crusades*, trans. Philip K. Hitti, New York, Columbia University Press, 1929

List of Illustrations

The *Capture of Constantinople by the Crusaders*, Eugène Delacroix, 19th century.

Index

Page numbers in italics refer to captions and/or illustrations.

Acknowledgments

The author and publisher wish to thank the following for their invaluable assistance: Sarab Atassi of the Institut Français d'Etudes Arabes in Damascus; Jacques Langade, director of the Institut Français d'Etudes Arabes in Damascus; and Mohammed Roumi. Michèle Decré-Cyssau oversaw the editorial production and coordination of this book. Catherine Letroquier designed the layout. Maud Fischer-Osostowicz was the photo editor. Dominique Guillaumin assembled the Documents. Patrick Mérienne made the maps on pages 27, 42, 71, and 103.

Photo Credits

All rights reserved front cover, 65l, 68b. Archives Nationales d'Outremer, Aix-en-Provence 167. Bibliothèque Municipale, Boulogne-sur-Mer 37a, 56, 57r. Bibliothèque Municipale, Lyons 36a, 40–1, 41a, 44r, 52a, 64b, 65r, 94, 95, 110. Biblioteca Nacional, Madrid 24–5a. Bibliothèque Nationale, Paris 13, 14, 16a, 17, 18al, 19, 23b, 30a, 34, 35, 37b, 38a, 38–9, 41b, 43, 44l, 45a, 45b, 56–7, 58b, 59a, 58–9, 60–1, 63, 64a, 66, 76, 78–9, 80–1a, 84, 84–5, 86l, 89, 90b, 92b, top, 93, 100, 100–1, 102–3, 106–7, 108, 109a, 109b, 110–1, 116–7, 117a, 118b, 118–9a, 121, 129, 130, 136, 139, 142, 149, 150, 153, 154–5, 158, 162, 164–5, 166, 167, 168–9, 171, 172, 178–9. Bodleian Library, Oxford 23a, 30–1, 54–5, 73a, 74al, 74ar, 74bl, 74br, 75, 97, 104–5, 112–3, 120–1, 174. British Library, London 18r, 33a, 77, 79a, 80–1b, 88–9, 91, 113a, 157. British Museum, London 98–9. Bulloz, Paris 134. Dagli Orti, Paris spine, 1, 16b, 22, 32, 72a, 83a. Gérard Degeorge, Paris 20–1. Edimédia, Paris 26, 117b, 137. E.R.L./Sipa Icono, Paris 33b, 82–3, 126–7. Explorer Archives, Paris 122–3a, 122b. Giraudon, Paris spine, 28–9, 31a, 36b, 52–3, 70–1, 98, 116b. A. F. Kersting, London 68–9, 69b, 72–3, 170, 186. E. Lessing/Magnum, Paris 53, 128. MAS, Barcelona 66–7. National Museum of Damascus/M. Roumi 61, 86–7a, 86–7c, 86–7b, 90a, 92b, center and below, 114–5, 126. Osterreichische Nationalbibliothek, Vienna 146. Rheinisches Landesmuseum, Bonn 28al, 28ar, 29al. Réunion des Musées Nationaux, Paris back cover, 2–3, 4–5, 8–9, 10–1, 46–7, 50–1, 70l, 92a, 124, 125, 177. Roger-Viollet, Paris 6–7, 48–9, 62, 133, 141, 143, 144, 159, 160, 161, 163. Scala, Florence 15, 29ar. Jean Vigne, Paris 96, 119b, 123b, 145, 147.

Text Credits

Grateful acknowledgment is made for use of material from the following works: *The Alexiad of Anna Comnena,* translated from the Greek by E. R. A. Sewter, Penguin Books Inc., 1969; copyright © 1969 E. R. A. Sewter (pp. 131–2, 158–9). *Arab Historians of the Crusades,* selected and translated from the Arabic sources by Francesco Gabrieli; translated from the Italian by E. J. Costello, Routledge & Kegan Paul Limited, London, 1969; English translation copyright © 1969 Routledge & Kegan Paul Limited (pp. 132–3, 135, 138–41, 148–9, 154–7, 159–61, 169). Bridge, Antony, *The Crusades,* Granada Publishing, 1980; copyright © 1980 Antony Bridge (p. 145). Brundage, James A., *Crusades: A Documentary Survey,* The Marquette University Press, Milwaukee, 1962 (pp. 136–7, 146–7). Fulcher of Chartres, *A History of the Expedition to Jerusalem: 1095–1127,* translated by Frances Rita Ryan, edited by Harold S. Fink, The University of Tennessee Press, Knoxville, 1969; copyright © 1969 The University of Tennessee Press (pp. 130–1). Goitein, S. D., "Contemporary Letters on the Capture of Jerusalem by the Crusaders," reproduced with the editor's permission from *Journal of Jewish Studies,* vol. 3, no. 4, 1952 (pp. 137–8). Le Goff, Jacques, *Medieval Civilization, 400–1500,* translated by Julia Barrow, Basil Blackwell Ltd, 1988; reprinted by permission of Basil Blackwell Ltd (pp. 175–6). Maalouf, Amin, *The Crusades through Arab Eyes,* translated by Jon Rothschild, Schocken Books, New York, 1985 (pp. 176–7). Prawer, Joshua, *The World of the Crusaders,* Weidenfeld and Nicolson, 1972; copyright © 1972 Joshua Prawer (pp. 142–5, 151–3). Runciman, Steven, *A History of the Crusades,* vol. 3, Cambridge University Press, 1954; reprinted with the permission of Cambridge University Press (pp. 162–5, 172–5). Smail, R. C., *Crusading Warfare (1097–1193),* Cambridge University Press, 1956; reprinted with the permission of Cambridge University Press (pp. 150–1).

Georges Tate studied at the Ecole Normale Supérieure of Saint-Cloud and received a doctorate in literature. From 1980 to 1990, he was director of the Institut Français d'Archéologie du Proche-Orient. Currently, he is director of the Archaeological Mission of Northern Syria and professor of ancient history at the university of Franche-Comté. A specialist in the East from the 3rd century BC to the 12th century AD, Georges Tate has published numerous articles on Syria's rural economy and society from Roman times to the Byzantine Empire. His book *Les Campagnes de la Syrie du Nord, du IIe au VIIe Siècle* was published in 1992.

For Jihane, Fabrice, and Aurélie.

Translated from the French by Lory Frankel

For Harry N. Abrams, Inc.
Editor: Sarah Burns
Typographic Designer: Elissa Ichiyasu
Design Supervisor: Miko McGinty
Assistant Designer: Tina Thompson
Text Permissions: Catherine Ruello

Library of Congress Catalog Card Number: 95–79941

ISBN 0–8109–2829–9

Published in 1996 by Harry N. Abrams, Inc., New York

Printed and bound in Italy by Editoriale Lloyd , Trieste